PUB WA

— IN —

Buckinghamshire

Trevor Yorke

COUNTRYSIDE BOOKS

NEWBURY, BERKSHIRE

COUNTRYSIDE BOOKS
3 Catherine Road
Newbury, Berkshire

To view our complete range of books,
please visit us at
www.countrysidebooks.co.uk

ISBN 1 85306 609 5

Designed by Graham Whiteman
Maps, photographs and illustrations by the author
Cover illustration by Colin Doggett

Produced through MRM Associates Ltd., Reading
Typeset by Techniset Typesetters, Newton-le-Willows
Printed by Woolnough Bookbinding Ltd., Irthlingborough

Contents

AREA MAP SHOWING LOCATIONS OF THE WALKS

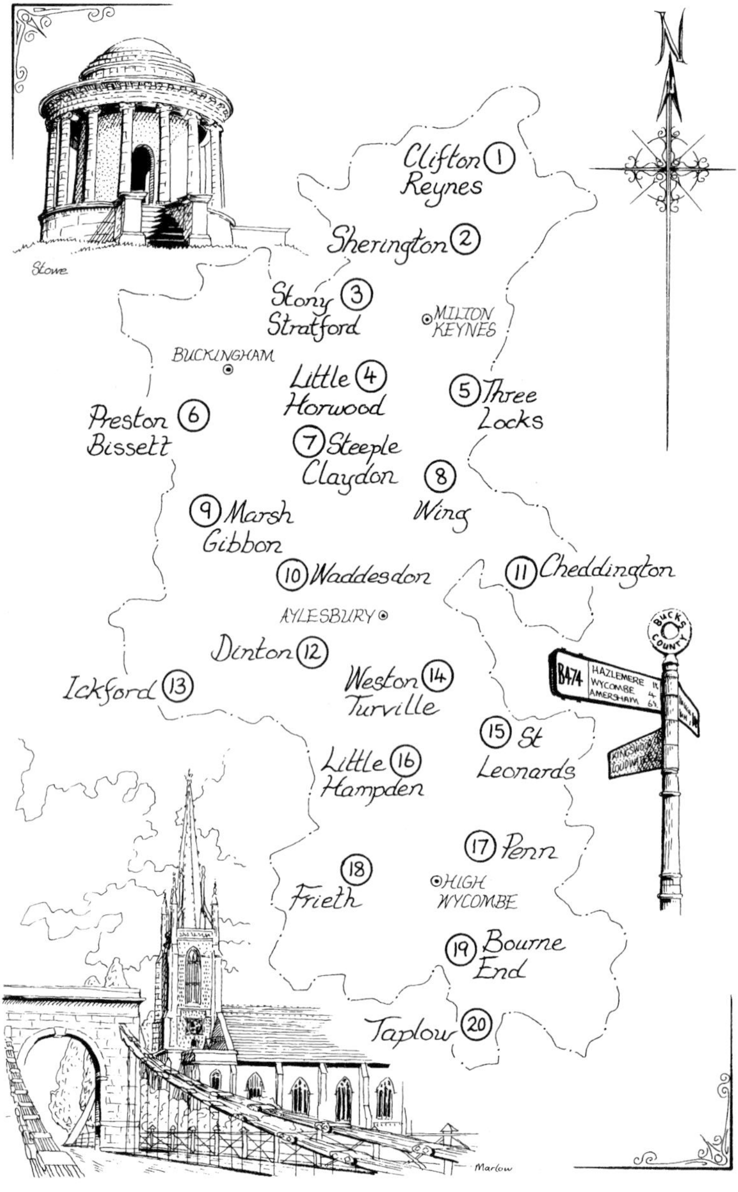

Stowe

N

Clifton Reynes ①

Sherington ②

Stony Stratford ③

⊙ MILTON KEYNES

BUCKINGHAM ⊙

Little Horwood ④

⑤ Three Locks

Preston Bissett ⑥

⑦ Steeple Claydon

⑧

Wing

⑨ Marsh Gibbon

⑩ Waddesdon

⑪ Cheddington

AYLESBURY ⊙

Dinton ⑫

Ickford ⑬

Weston Turville ⑭

B474 HAZLEMERE WYCOMBE AMERSHAM

⑮ St Leonards

Little Hampden ⑯

⑰ Penn

⑱ Frieth

⊙ HIGH WYCOMBE

⑲ Bourne End

Taplow ⑳

Marlow

Walk

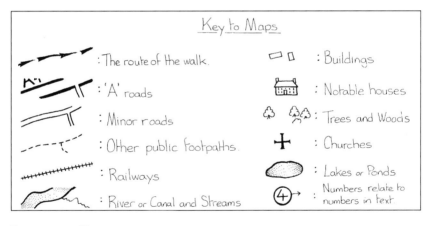

PUBLISHER'S NOTE

We hope that you obtain considerable enjoyment from this book; great care has been taken in its preparation. However, changes of landlord and actual closures are sadly not uncommon. Likewise, although at the time of publication all routes followed public rights of way or permitted paths, diversion orders can be made and permissions withdrawn.

We cannot of course, be held responsible for such diversion orders and any inaccuracies in the text which result from these or any other changes to the routes nor any damage which might result from walkers trespassing on private property. We are anxious though that all details covering the walks and the pubs are kept up to date and would therefore welcome information from readers which would be relevant to future editions.

INTRODUCTION

Buckinghamshire is a long finger of a county and is composed of horizontal bands of varying geology. This, coupled with an ever-increasing distance from London the further north you go, determines the environment and social structure of the towns and villages. Nowhere is this more obvious than in the public house.

In the south of the county, where the beech-clad hills of the Chilterns have long attracted city folk, villages are dominated by the commuter and the retired. The public houses in these communities have changed perceptibly to cater for this market, many concentrating on their restaurants or at least offering a good selection of food. Some may lament the ever-decreasing cosy local, but for the visitor the standard of the surviving pubs is excellent.

Once you head north over the chalk escarpment you enter the Aylesbury Vale where the influence of the train and motorway have only a mild effect. The pubs are often genuinely ancient establishments which provide food and drink for all comers without turning their back on the local trade.

As you reach the northerly limits of the county you enter the Midlands with limestone buildings and gently rolling hills where agriculture still holds sway. Here in contrast to the south the pubs serve vibrant communities which retain shops, garages and schools, and in my experience are all the more welcoming to the stranger.

I set myself the challenge with this book to discover some of these more remote areas whilst keeping an even distribution of walks across the county. There will hopefully be a good selection of locations within 20 or so miles of wherever you are in Buckinghamshire. The routes are all circular and traverse all manner of landscapes. From the wide river valley at Clifton Reynes to the beechwoods around Frieth and from the boggy flats at Marsh Gibbon to the canals at Cheddington and Three Locks. There are grand houses to visit, humble cottages to admire and where possible another pub halfway round for the impatient! All the walks are between 2$^{1}/_{2}$ and 5 miles in length and avoid serious ups and downs (except a few in the Chilterns), but you will encounter muddy patches and, even for Taplow where the paths are tarmacked, I would recommend wearing walking boots or stout shoes (and removing them before entering the pub!).

The sketch maps are intended to guide you to the pub and give you a simple yet accurate idea of the walk route. I have also included the numbers of the relevant Ordnance Survey sheets (Landranger 1:50 000 or Explorer 1:25 000) for each walk — these are especially recommended for identifying the main features of views.

Despite my best efforts to ensure that the featured pubs' facilities and menus cater for all the family, the fluctuating nature of the brewing industry means that there will inevitably be changes (often for the better). If in doubt then telephone to enquire before setting out. It goes without saying, of course, that the pub car parks are for the use of customers — and you should always check that leaving your car there when you set out on your walk is not a problem. I have also suggested alternative parking places.

Finally, may I wish you many happy outings in the lovely Buckinghamshire countryside, but most of all I hope you enjoy the thrill of discovery that I felt when visiting, for instance, the White Hart at Sherington. This pub is hidden up a back lane in a long since bypassed village yet to my surprise inside it opened out into what is best described as a medieval hall offering service that would have satisfied royalty. What more could one ask?

Trevor Yorke

① Clifton Reynes
The Robin Hood

The walk passes through the pasture and meadows around the River Ouse then along Olney's tree-lined High Street, flanked with historic stone buildings. Despite the flat countryside there are good views from the B565 and from the hill by Clifton Reynes towards Olney and its distinctive church spire.

Clifton Reynes is a secluded hamlet strung along a dead-end lane leading up to the 13th-century church, which, as the name 'Clifton' suggests, stands towards the top of a steep drop to the River Ouse and Olney below. This town, once the centre of the Buckinghamshire lace-making industry, is now better known as the home of the famous poet William Cowper who, along with the slave trader turned rector John Newton, wrote the 'Olney Hymns' in the 1770s. The Cowper Museum in the Market Place houses original manuscripts. The tree-lined High Street and the church by the river make Olney a popular place, in contrast to Clifton where the only visitors are those to the Robin Hood.

Do not be fooled by the plain, pebble dashed exterior of this surprisingly large pub. As soon as you enter (but don't forget to leave any muddy boots in the porch) you find a snug lounge with inglenook fireplaces. Beyond it is a light and airy conservatory with a spectacular grapevine overhead. Outside, the lawn sweeps up the slope with fields beyond. These features make the pub an attractive proposition come summer or winter. Children are welcome in the garden or the conservatory.

Greene King beers are served on handpump and there is a good collection of wines. The menu is impressive, with pan fried duck breast with redcurrant sauce and home-made potato-topped fisherman's pie among the mouthwatering main courses. There is also vegetarian food as well as ploughman's, basket meals and sandwiches (please note that the selection is more limited on Sundays). The opening times are 12 noon to 2.30 pm and 6.30 pm to 11 pm. Food is served from 12 noon to 2 pm and 7 pm to 9.30 pm on Tuesday to Saturday and from 12 noon to 2 pm only on Sunday (no food on Mondays).

Telephone: 01234 711574.

- **HOW TO GET THERE:** From Milton Keynes either take the A422 off the A5 towards Wellingborough or the A509 from junction 14 on the M1 which joins the A422 just north of Newport Pagnell. Carry on towards Wellingborough and after 4 miles and just before Emberton take a right turn signposted to Clifton Reynes. Follow this minor road (watch out for the sharp left bend after only a hundred yards) for 2 miles until reaching a T junction where you turn left into the village. The Robin Hood is on your left.
- **PARKING:** There are some spaces at the front of the pub, otherwise park along the roadside, being careful not to block any accesses.
- **LENGTH OF THE WALK:** 3¹/₂ miles. Map: OS Landranger 152 Northampton and Milton Keynes (GR 902512).

THE WALK

1. Stand with your back to the pub and cross the main village road, continuing up the lane opposite. This tarmac road takes you out of the village and then makes a sharp left turn where there is a footpath sign informing you that you are on the Three Shires Way. Carry on along the road and over the railway bridge. This crosses the old Bedford to Northampton Railway which brought new prosperity to Olney in the 1870s. Down the other side the tarmac road turns right into a farm but you carry on along the rough track ahead. This leads you down in a

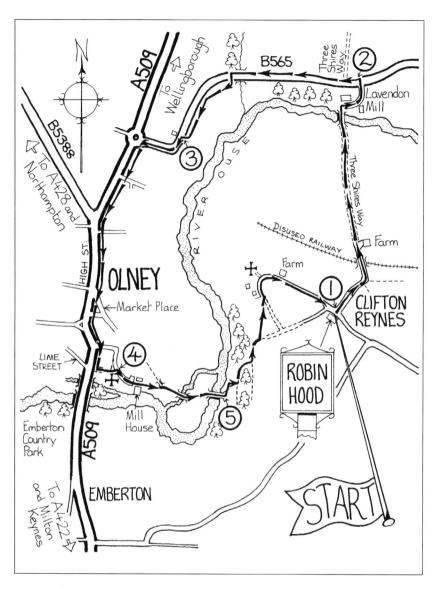

straight line to the river which you cross on the bridge in front of the old mill buildings. Once over go across the grass up to the main building then turn right up the gravel drive to the main road.

2. Turn left along the B road (walk on the right-hand side) and follow it for ¼ mile (I crossed over when the road started to go downhill as the verge is wider on the left and there are pleasant views to be had over the Ouse Valley). At the bottom of the drop there is a small red-bricked bridge and just after it a gap in the hedge on your left. Pass through this gap and head along the path in the direction of the footpath sign, which cuts off the sharp corner of the road. The path meets the road at the other side of the field, but you cross over the stile in front and walk along the hedge, parallel to the road.

3. At the end of this field you rejoin the road and, keeping to the wider left-hand verge, follow it round the right-hand bend and up to the roundabout. Turn left here and follow the main road for the next mile through Olney. Look out for the old shoe factory with its curved glass windows, the Castle Inn which is reputedly haunted and the Cowper Museum which dominates the Market Place.

Past the Market Place you keep to the main road down towards the bridge. Just before you reach it and opposite Lime Street, turn left up the path into the churchyard and follow it along the left-hand side of the church and out the other side onto the back road. This edifice was built between 1325 and 1350 with a huge broach spire. If you look back from the bridge when you reach point 5 you can see right through the spire!

4. Turn right and down the lane which presently ends. Carry on along the tarmac bridleway which runs straight ahead, going between the buildings and then through the gate at the bottom. Keep to the path which runs parallel to the river and then go through the next gate whereupon another path joins you from the left. Cross the small bridge ahead and follow what has now become a stone path up to the bridge over the Ouse.

5. Once over the bridge turn immediately left then right, then the stone path ends at a T junction. Turn left up the paving stone path which leads you to a clearing with no obvious route. Go straight up the grassy slope ahead and at the top you will find a small path running along the ridge. Turn left and follow it as it curves up to the right-hand corner of the field and a gate. Just before this there is a stile in the fence on your left. Cross this stile and walk towards the right of the two buildings on the other side of the field where you will find a gate at the end of the stone wall. Pass through it and turn left down the lane past the rectory and St Mary's church then follow the lane as it turns right and takes you back to the Robin Hood.

② Sherington
The White Hart

Despite there being no noticeable climbs there are excellent views to be had over the winding River Ouse and beyond. The return journey is through the Tyringham Hall estate with its splendid church and bridge.

Sherington stands on the gently rolling hills that overlook the Ouse Valley. Two great houses stand either side of the river to the west of the village, Tyringham and Gayhurst. Both houses are private and were built for two notable men. The former was for William Praed, MP, who became the first chairman of the nearby Grand Junction Canal while the rebuilding of Gayhurst was completed for Sir Everard Digby. Digby was noted around the court for his good looks and sweetness of character, but to everyone's surprise became involved in the Gunpowder Plot of 1605. At his execution his heart was ripped out to the shout of 'here is the heart of a traitor', to which Digby is said to have gasped 'thou liest', despite the physical impossibility of such an act!

Sherington is now a peaceful working village with a picturesque green overlooked by an imposing garage. At the other end of Church Road is an idyllic setting of old stone houses and cottages with the White Hart tucked behind them. The pub is approached from a narrow courtyard with old brick stables and a huge horse chestnut tree casting dappled light over the 17th-century stone building. Through the doorway is the central bar with drinking areas on either side and seating in both bay windows. There is a fireplace to the right but most notably to the left is the dining area. You drop down a few steps into what can be best described as a medieval hall! The high beamed ceiling and tall stone walls with wine racks set in alcoves make it a most charismatic place to eat. The garden at the rear can be accessed from inside the pub or around the outside and provides seating under trees or along the attractive new terrace. This freehouse has an ever-changing selection of beers on handpump including Notley, Wychert, Jennings and Frog Island! An equally excellent range of food is offered on blackboards from mouthwatering meat and vegetarian dishes to chunky sandwiches and bowls of chips. The opening times are from 11 am to 3 pm and 6 pm to 11 pm (10.30 pm on Sundays).

The perfect setting and the building itself are enough to make this a good pub, the food and beer make it truly memorable.

Telephone: 01908 617591.

- **HOW TO GET THERE:** From Milton Keynes or junction 14 on the M1 take the A509 north towards Wellingborough. A few miles north of the M1 you turn right at a roundabout where the A509 joins the A422 and becomes dual carriageway. At the next roundabout turn left to Sherington and after $1/4$ mile turn right into the village. At the crossroads in the middle by the shop, turn right up Church Road until you reach a green on your right and your second left turn is Gun Lane. The White Hart is immediately on your left.
- **PARKING:** There is very limited parking in front of the pub so it may be best to park around the top of Church Road by the green.
- **LENGTH OF THE WALK:** 5 miles. Maps: OS Pathfinder 1024 or Landranger 152 Northampton and Milton Keynes (GR 891468).

THE WALK

1. With your back to the pub turn left and walk up Gun Lane and out of the village. When you reach the T junction turn right and at the second gate immediately on your left is a footpath sign and stile. Cross over this

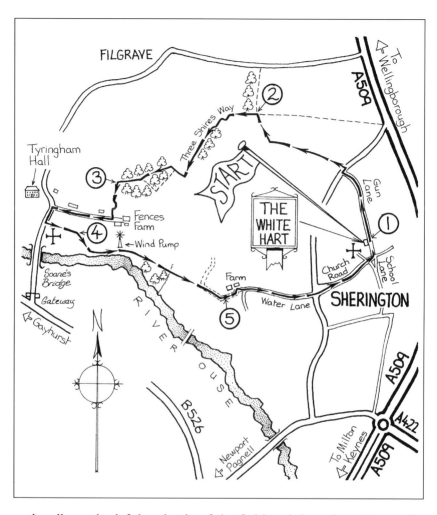

and walk up the left-hand side of the field and then down into a dip where the path turns 45 degrees right by a V-shaped new plantation of oaks. This takes you towards a clump of trees on top of the hill.

2. At the top turn left in front of the gateway and walk along the right-hand edge of the field. There are plenty of good views along this stretch across the Ouse Valley and over Milton Keynes to the hills beyond. In summer you may be surprised to see dragonflies in these fields – the larger ones can roam far from water. These pretty insects are less appealing in their earlier nymph form when they are ferocious carnivores spearing prey with their spiky jaws!

After a short while the path turns right and through a gateway. Go through this then turn left and walk along the right-hand side of the hedge and the strip of woodland beyond. As the field starts to drop down there is another gate where you turn right and walk along the right-hand side of the new hedge up to the corner of the wood at the top. When you reach the trees you will see a gap a few yards up the right-hand side which you go through and then continue along the path which winds through the middle of the wood. Ignore the paths to your left and this will take you up to a gate at the far side of the wood.

3. Go through the gate, turn 45 degrees left and walk along the hedge on the right. It goes round a square clump of scrub and then in the corner you will see a gate by the nearest of the tall poplar trees. Go through this and turn right and then left through the gate beside the house and onto a concrete drive. Turn right and walk along it all the way to the junction with the road. Turn left along the edge of the road with Tyringham Hall in the trees to your right. Before you reach the church in the trees there is a bridleway sign by a gate; turn left here and walk along the fence on the left-hand side of the field beyond. Carry on along the fence through a gateway and up to a hedge with a stile.

If time allows continue along the road before turning along the bridleway and have a look at the church and if you walk behind it you get a good view of the graceful bridge built by John Soane 200 years ago. The gateway beyond, also by Soane, has been designated as being of European architectural importance!

4. Over the stile you turn slightly right and head diagonally down to the trees and then walk along the edge of the river and through another gate. Carry on up to and past the windpump and through the gate beyond it. Walk along the row of trees on your right up to another gate under a large chestnut. In the next field walk along the right-hand side beside a ditch with a few pollarded willows until, passing through gateposts, you join a track which comes in from your left. Carry on in the same direction up to a gate set diagonally in front of you.

5. Turn 45 degrees left in front of the gate and this takes you up to a farmhouse, then left into the yard where you keep right to reach the concrete drive at the entrance to the farm. Go up the left-hand leg of the drive along the hedge on your left and this turns into a tarmac road (Water Lane) which leads you all the way back into the centre of the village. At the crossroads go straight across and walk up Church Road to return to Gun Lane and the White Hart.

3 Stony Stratford
The Old George Hotel

An excellent walk to dispel any ideas that the Milton Keynes area is boring! You start among imposing Georgian buildings and visit two peaceful hamlets composed of rustic stone cottages and houses. In between are riverside pastures and parkland while the return is via the surprising Horsefair Green.

Stony Stratford is an island of historic buildings in the sea of modernity which laps at its shore. The original settlement was north of the River Ouse where Watling Street crossed (Stratford is Saxon for 'ford on a Roman road'). The present town was laid out in the 12th century, with the former site being renamed Old Stratford. Richard III is said to have captured the 'Young Princes' in 1483 at an inn on the opposite side of the High Street from the Old George, and a plaque now marks the spot.

The first turnpike road in England ran from here to Hockcliffe in 1725 and heralded a boom time with the building of numerous coaching inns and hotels. The two largest of these are the Cock and the Bull from which the saying 'a Cock and Bull story' is said to originate!

Another reason for the many Georgian frontages was a series of fires, the greatest of which in 1742 destroyed 146 houses and St Mary's church (its tower is still standing down an alleyway just north of the Cock). In the Market Square is the stump of an old elm, in the shelter of which John Wesley is said to have preached. He found the people 'Stony by name and Stony by nature', though thankfully you will find the opposite today when you visit the Old George.

The building dates back to the early 1600s and entry is strangely down steps between the two large bay windows. The richly coloured interior maintains the ancient character of the inn. A good range of handpumped beers is offered from the spacious bar and there is an extensive menu with 'Specials of the Day' and 'The George Burger' being of note. There are vegetarian meals and a two-course Sunday roast is also served. Best still, food is available all day! The opening times are from 11 am to 11 pm, seven days a week.

Telephone: 01908 562181.

- **HOW TO GET THERE:** From the centre of Milton Keynes take the A5 dual carriageway north until after about 3 miles it ends at a roundabout. Take the first left off the roundabout down Towcester Road, over the traffic lights and the River Ouse. Immediately after the bridge turn right down the High Street where you will find the Old George at the far end.
- **PARKING:** There are spaces along the High Street although the parking times may be limited. There is also a car park in the Market Square. Both options may be full at busy shopping times, when you will have to look around the numerous back streets.
- **LENGTH OF THE WALK:** 3½ miles. Maps: OS Explorer 192 Buckingham and Milton Keynes and Pathfinder 1023 (both are needed) or Landranger 152 Northampton and Milton Keynes (GR 788404).

THE WALK

1. With your back to the Old George turn left and walk up as far as the Bull then go left down Church Street. This ends at the corner of Market Square where you turn right along an unnamed back lane. Market Square is surrounded by some fine Georgian houses with the ancient stump of the Wesley Tree in the centre. Down the back lane and just past York Road is a footpath sign pointing to a tree-lined tarmac path. Turn left and follow this path until, passing through a rough area with piles of rubble, you emerge at the entrance to the Ouse Valley Park.

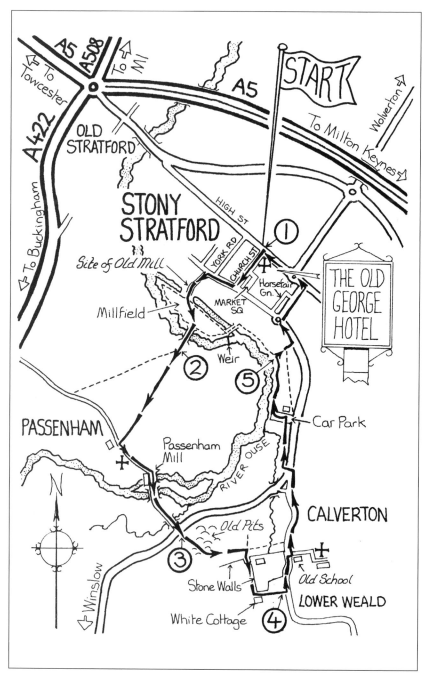

The piles of rubble are all that remain of the old mill which was destroyed in 1985. Take the middle path by the information board which is signposted to Passenham and crosses Millfield, up to the bridge on the other side. The pollarded tree stumps to your left that bend around the play area mark the line of the old river before its new course was cut in 1955. Go over the bridge and up to the gate beyond.

2. The path forks here and you take the left-hand one which heads straight across the field in front of you in the direction of Passenham church tower. Keep in a straight line, pass through another gate and then cross the next field until you reach the road just to the right of the church. Turn left down the lane, past St Guthlac's with its odd barrel-roofed chancel and then over the river in front of Passenham Mill. Keep to the pretty lane until you get to the T junction with the Stratford to Winslow road.

3. Slightly to the right on the other side of the road is a footpath sign; cross over and go through the hedge here. On the other side you will find you are surrounded by a series of pits (probably old local stone workings). Head towards them in the exact direction of the footpath sign. This will take you over a narrow causeway through the undulations, roughly parallel to the hedge on your right, until you reach a high point where the pits end. On the other side of the field is a brick and stone wall and just past its left-hand end you can see a footpath sign. Cross the field to it and then turn right and cross the stile at the left-hand end of the aforementioned wall. Go past the house on your left and then follow the stone wall which runs along a dip down to a white thatched cottage. At the cottage turn left, through the tight gap between it and the wall, down the gravel path, over the stream and up to the road.

4. Turn left and follow the pavement out of Lower Weald and into the equally tiny Calverton. Cross over by the Old School and keep along the pavement on the other side. If time allows have a look at the elaborate church and the brick almshouses to the side with their odd little top windows. Back along the road you pass the Shoulder of Mutton and then join the main Stratford to Winslow road. As the pavement ends by the seat, cross over and go through the fence at the footpath sign. Go right and walk up this narrow strip of grass until you reach the small car park. You could step back onto the road here and follow it on to Horsefair Green but I prefer to go round the back of the brick building and follow the path alongside the River Ouse. Go over the small bridge then after another 50 yards or so you reach a fence.

Calverton Place

5. If you carry on along the path by the river then it will lead you back to Millfield. I suggest, though, turning right just before this fence and walking across the field up to a gap in the fence in the top corner which takes you back onto Calverton Road. Turn left and then at the mini roundabout go right and walk up the charming Horsefair Green. At the top turn left past the roundabout and back along the High Street to the Old George Hotel.

Little Horwood
The Shoulder of Mutton

4

This walk takes you around the oldest parts of the village and then across fields to Horwood House. There are ancient houses, modern mansions, fields and woods of rich variety, and an old station with a unique piece of hedge cutting!

'Horwudu' as the village was known twelve hundred years ago means 'filthy wood'! Today things have changed; there is barely any woodland and Little Horwood is a pristine collection of tidy timber and brick cottages. The trees that remain surround thatch and slated houses, some dating back four hundred years, set around a small green. At the north end of the village is St Nicholas's church with a tower made of huge blocks of limestone which is best viewed from the garden of its neighbour, the Shoulder of Mutton.

The pub building dates back in part to the 15th century and its mix of black and white timber-frame and thatched brick retains this antique feel. Once inside, this aura is further enhanced by the tiled floor, low beams and inglenook fireplace. The small L-shaped bar stands opposite french doors which lead onto the pièce de résistance, the garden. Set on a gentle grass slope with trees and benches it is open to fields on one side and over-looked by the aforementioned church on the other.

Everyone, including dogs, are welcome in the garden, which can be accessed directly from the car park through the black timber barn. Inside the pub you will find Pedigree and ABC on handpump with a selection of wines and spirits. The food is all homecooked and includes vegetarian meals and children's portions, and the steak and kidney pie is of particular note. There is a wide choice of sandwiches and sweets, and meals come served with the usual choice of accompaniments including the faithful chip! Opening times are from 11 am to 2.30 pm and 6 pm to 11 pm on weekdays (closed Monday lunchtime). On Saturday the times are 11 am to 3 pm and 6 pm to 11 pm while on Sunday the pub is open from 12 noon to 3 pm and 7 pm to 10.30 pm. Telephone: 01296 712514.

- **HOW TO GET THERE:** Little Horwood is 2 miles north-east of Winslow. Approaching from Aylesbury, head up the A413 towards Buckingham and just as you enter Winslow turn right by the 30 mph signs to Little Horwood. After going under a railway bridge and past a mile or so of fields you enter the village. The pub is at the far end, just past the church.
- **PARKING:** There is a car park alongside the pub. Alternatively there is plenty of room to park on Mursley Road in the middle of the village.
- **LENGTH OF THE WALK:** 3½ miles. Maps: OS Explorer 192 Buckingham and Milton Keynes or Landranger 165 Aylesbury and Leighton Buzzard (GR 790309).

THE WALK

1. From the pub head back towards the village along the short grey stone wall retaining the churchyard. At its end turn left through the church gates and take the right-hand tarmac path along the side of the churchyard. At the rear you go through a gap in the tall fence and then past the right-hand side of the school building to emerge in the sports field. Head towards the top right corner by the trees where you will find a stile. If you feel daring you can cross the little stream in the trees and find the old moat beyond. This used to surround a grand house but by the beginning of the 20th century it was reduced to a decaying farmhouse. Now it is half buried in undergrowth.

2. Once over the stile keep to the fence and trees on your right and

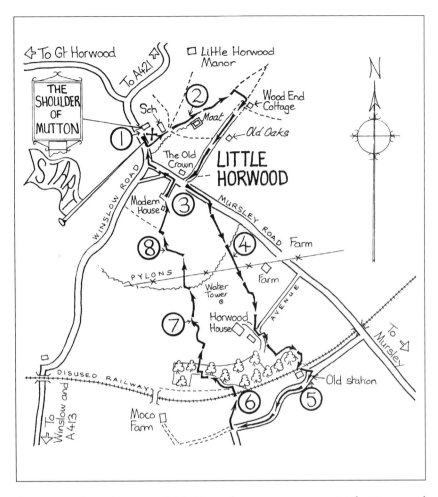

then cross into the next field. From here you can see Little Horwood Manor on the hill to the left. It was only finished in 1939, making it one of the last mansions built in England. Carry on along the hedge until it makes a sharp right turn. Do the same and walk up to the crossroads of fences by the black and white house (Wood End Cottage). Turn right again here, over two stiles and onto the lane which you follow back into the village. Just opposite the first house on the right is Old Oaks, a rare jettied 16th-century house.

3. This lane called Wood End, emerges onto Mursley Road by the Old Crown pub. Turn left and walk up the right-hand side of the road out of the village. Just past the last house on the right is a gate and footpath sign. Go through the gate and head diagonally across the field in the direction indicated by the sign (halfway between the farm buildings and the water tower on the horizon). You should see a stile in the hedge ahead which you cross along with the little bridge beyond. Then, carrying on in the same direction, you go towards the metal gate beside the larger oak tree in this next field.

4. Go through this gate and on the same line head towards the far corner of the field, under the pylons, over a manhole cover and finally to the stiles in the trees beyond. Traverse these and turn left and over the gate in front to find yourself in the grounds of Horwood House. Turn and walk in a straight line towards the main house. To help you cross the electric fences which block this public footpath there are blue hoses on the top wires followed by two conventional stiles. This will put you on the road which runs around the building. The original Horwood House was demolished and replaced by this building in 1912. It is now a training centre hence the large carbuncle which has been attached to it!

Turn left along the wall in front of the house (ignore the road in an avenue of trees to your left) and then just as the wall ends on your right you cross over a stile in the fence on your left. Once in the field turn right and follow the perimeter fence down to the wood and then left, round a bend until you find a stile with an arrow disc on. Cross this, go over a bridge and the stile beyond, then turn right and continue along the wood edge until, just before the railway you turn right into the trees. Go over another bridge and towards the picket gate which once you pass through leads you up onto the old railway station.

Look for the footpath sign to the left of the station house and cross the tracks towards it. This is the old Oxford to Cambridge railway which had trains running on it up until a few years ago. The station is now a private residence but it seems fitting that the hedge at the front has been cut into the shape of a steam engine!

5. Once on the road turn right and follow it around the rear of the station's garden and then on for a $1/4$ mile until it makes a sharp left turn. Ignore the track in front to Moco Farm, and turn right through the gate and head towards the metal gate to the left of the mound on the other side of the field. Pass through the gate and go along the path through the trees up to the railway which you cross again.

6. From the railway head straight across towards the wood then before reaching it turn left and follow its perimeter for a few hundred yards until a stile and bridge appear. Turn right over them, then left on

The 'Topiary Loco' at Swanbourne Station

entering the wood and follow the arrows to the stile on the other side. Notice the wide variety of trees from pine, birch and larch to willow, horse chestnut and ash. You will now be looking at the rear of Horwood House. Cross the stile and walk up the left-hand side of the field until, just before it meets the wooden fence, there is a gap which you pass through. In the next field walk up the right-hand side as the fence zigzags up to the top of the hill.

7. Go over the stile and then right along the edge of the next field until the trees you are walking beside turn right towards the water tower. You carry straight on, across the field and down to a clump of trees in the hedge at the bottom. Here you will find a gap and beyond it another bridge and stile to cross. Once over these turn right again and walk up the side of this field. At the top turn left along the hedge until just before the next corner you cross over a stile to your right.

8. About 45 degrees to your left is another stile, which you cross, then turn right and go over the stile in the fence in front. Cross the field by heading for the right-hand side of the cream and brown modern house then pass along the grassy track around the edge of its garden. This takes you up to the end of a cul-de-sac, where you turn right back to Mursley Road by the Old Crown. Turn left down past the green and then right at the bottom and back up to the Shoulder of Mutton.

Three Locks
The Three Locks

A unique area of Buckinghamshire with sandy heathland, mixed woodland and marshy fields scattered with ponds. There is an easy start along the canal then a climb over Furze Hill with views down the Ouzel Valley. Oak Wood is the highlight with an enchanting mix of deciduous and coniferous trees.

The three locks which drop the Grand Union Canal twenty feet on its way down the Ouzel Valley, give the name and reason for the pub which overlooks them. The canal was constructed 200 years ago as a short cut between the Midlands and London. It was built with double locks to encourage wider barges but the connecting canals still had singles so only narrowboats could ever use it. Water shortage was always a problem here and the first answer was to build single locks parallel to the present double ones. The remains of one of these can be seen in front of the pumping station which is the most recent way of moving water back up the flight. The other method was to use side pounds where water could be collected and used to fill locks rather than drawing the precious water from the pound above.

It is in one of these dried outside pounds that outdoor seating is provided for visitors to the Three Locks pub. The building is almost as old as the canal and was a popular stop off for boaters who would fill up their flagons while passing through the locks. Other visitors are the ghosts of a woman, and child in a pram, who are believed to have drowned in the lock. Occupants have claimed to have heard the squeaking of the pram wheels! The picturesque exterior is maintained inside with beamed ceiling and wood-planked floor. Behind the spacious bar are Speckled Hen and Marston's Pedigree on handpump and a good selection of wines and spirits. Home-cooked food is another attraction and includes braised knuckle of lamb, vegetarian harvester's pie and 'The Chef's Curry of the Day'. The extensive menu also offers jacket potatoes, sandwiches and the humble chip! This is a traditional pub which is convenient for all the family. The opening times are from 12 noon to 11 pm in the summer and from 12 noon to 2.30 pm and 6 pm to 11 pm in the winter.

Telephone: 01525 270470.

- **HOW TO GET THERE:** From Milton Keynes head south on the A5 dual carriageway and turn right down the A4146 to Leighton Buzzard. Follow the road for a few miles, pass through Stoke Hammond and then about $1/2$ mile after the village you will see the white building of the pub and the three locks on your left.
- **PARKING:** There is space in the lay-by alongside the pub, but the best spot is probably the car park by the bridge.
- **LENGTH OF THE WALK:** $3^1/2$ miles. Maps: OS Explorer 192 Buckingham and Milton Keynes or Landranger 165 Aylesbury and Leighton Buzzard (GR 891284).

THE WALK

1. From the front of the pub go down past the bottom lock and along the towpath, which follows the left-hand side of the canal for the next $1/2$ mile. At the first bridge go up and over it but rather than following the canal carry straight on along the tarmac drive through the entrance to Paper Mill Farm. The drive takes you around the old mill, over the River Ouzel and then becomes just a rough track as it starts to climb. After 100 yards you reach a cluster of barns where the track forks and you take the right-hand option which carries on uphill alongside the hedge.

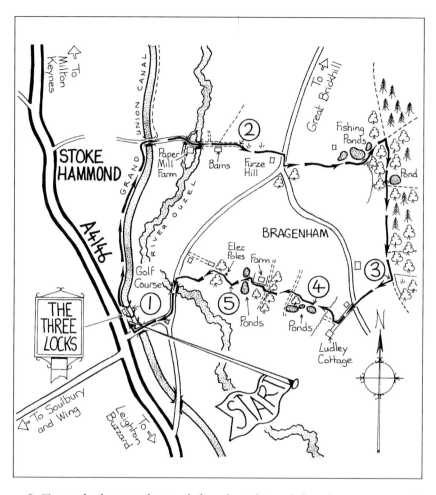

2. Towards the top the track bends right and then becomes a path which winds through the sandy heathland between wire fences. These hills are known as the Greensand Ridge from the sandstone which contains glauconite, giving it a green tinge. When it is weathered, as it is here, on the surface this colouring isn't noticeable but the change of flora is, with gorse, bracken and birch predominant.

The path takes you around Furze Hill House and onto its tarmac drive which you follow down to the road. Turn right and almost immediately cross over and go down the bridleway at the road junction with Bragenham Lane. Follow this route as it winds down past a cluster of ponds and then up into the woods beyond. After a few hundred yards and as the bridleway levels off you reach a crossroads with a sign where you turn right down 'Bucks Circular Walk'. This woodland has a wonderful mix of trees, mainly oak but with sweet chestnut, lime, birch, maple, hazel, pines and firs. The path winds through the trees down to a pond where, after you cross a tiny stream, you take the right-hand path (virtually straight ahead). This follows the edge of the wood for a few hundred yards, ignoring a path turning off; you then reach a fenced-off enclosure on your left.

3. On your right opposite the enclosure is a stile in the hedge. Go over this and cross the field, veering slightly left. As you go over the brow of the hill you will see a clump of grass with a post in down near the edge of the field. Head for this (notice the arrow on the post) and just behind it in the fence are a stile and steps which take you down to the road.

The return journey from here is along a little-used footpath which can be vague in parts. There are arrows on stiles and electricity posts which are generally accurate in their direction. Go straight over the road and down the track past the house and then, before reaching Ludley Cottage, turn right by the footpath sign along the fir tree hedge. After only 10 to 20 yards there is a post with an arrow on and you turn about 30 degrees to your right and cross through the marshy area of tall grass up to a stile. Over this turn right in the direction of the arrow and then bend left round a tree and over a plank bridge. Go straight across the field beyond in a line between the hedge on your left and the line of electricity poles on the right. This takes you up to a stile above the first of numerous ponds.

4. Over the stile you walk between the fence and hedge, go over another stile, ignore the gap on your right and carry on between the fence and bush with the ponds still down to your left. This takes you up to a large tree by a stile which you cross and in the direction of the arrow go over the next field to the stile beyond. Over this you turn about 30 degrees to your left and cross towards the corner fencepost with another arrow. Continue past it and on to the stile by the gate. The arrow on this one guides you down to the edge of a wood where you find another stile to cross. Once over turn immediately right and then left over a plank bridge and on in the same direction until you go up a small bank and out of the trees.

This leaves you in a patch of rough ground with a red-brick farmhouse to your right. There is an electricity pole with an arrow on it to the left of the gate to the house. Head towards and past this pole and

29

The Grand Union Canal at Three Locks

follow the path as it then runs along the farm wall on your right. At the end it turns 90 degrees and then ends at a stile in the fence on your left. Over this you head between the two ponds in the field and then, turning slightly left and away from the line of the electricity poles, go across to a corner fencepost with another arrow on it.

5. Now turn to your right in the direction of the arrow and head over the boggy ground back to the next electricity pole and then onwards in the direction of the arrow on it. This takes you into some low scrubby trees and then up to a fence on their far edge. Turn right and walk, still within the trees, until you find a stile in the fence. Go over this and head for the gap in the fence on your left, then turn and head for the bottom right corner of the field. Just before you reach it there is a stile which you cross and then walk along the right of the hedge as it curves round to the left. As another hedge comes in on your right you will see a gate and stile. Go over these and turn left along the road which you follow all the way back (ignoring the left-hand fork) to the Three Locks.

6 Preston Bissett
The White Hart

A gentle stroll over a pastoral landscape dominated by ancient buildings: Chetwode's Elizabethan manor house and the Old Priory Church, and even the humble edifice in Preston Bissett are of note. Also look out for ancient moats, strange banks and ditches and an old well head lost in the trees!

Preston Bissett and its near neighbour Chetwode are historically linked: Preston means 'priest's town or farm' and there was an ancient priory at Chetwode. The name of the latter is also rare in that it is made up of two parts both meaning the same thing, 'a wood'! The first part is Ancient British and the second Saxon, which indicates habitation dating back to Roman times. The family of the same name used to collect Rhyne Tax from the villagers who were indebted to a 12th-century lord, John Chetwode, for killing a huge wild boar which had been terrorising the area. When a mound known as 'Boars Pond' at nearby Barton Hartshorn was excavated in 1810, bones of an unusually large animal fitting its description were found!

The old priory was dissolved in 1460 and its church was granted to the villagers but an argument with the Lord of the Manor led to him demolishing half of the building. All that remains today is the old chancel with a later tower built on the front.

Preston Bissett has had a less dramatic history dependent on agriculture. The schoolchildren were even allowed time off for 'potato picking, blackberrying, threshing and crow scaring'! The White Hart has served this farming community for over 300 years and it still retains its original features. From the black and white timber-framed walls and thatched roof to the low-beamed interior, it oozes character. Behind the bar you will find a wide range of beers, wines, malts and even elderflower spritzer! The menu is mouthwatering. How about 'steamed mussels in white wine and cream' or 'goat's cheese crostini on a bed of mixed leaves'? Even the potatoes are Aga baked!

There is some seating in the yard outside this delightful pub and a few parking spaces at the rear. The opening times are 12 noon to 2.30 pm and 6.30 pm to 11 pm on Monday to Saturday and 12 noon to 3 pm and 7 pm to 10.30 pm on Sunday (no food on Tuesday lunchtime).

Telephone: 01280 847969.

- **HOW TO GET THERE:** From Bicester take the old A421 (now A4421) to Buckingham or vice versa. Next to the railway bridge in Newton Purcell is a turning to Preston Bissett. Go down here through Barton Hartshorn and then turn left at the T junction. Take the first right turn after a few hundred yards and proceed down this road for about a mile. At the end turn right towards Preston Bissett and then after a bend take the first left up Bushes Lane. Just before the nurseries turn right down Pound Lane and you will find the White Hart on the right just after entering the village.
- **PARKING:** There is room along the roadside past the pub.
- **LENGTH OF THE WALK:** 3 miles. Maps: OS Explorer 192 Buckingham and Milton Keynes or Landranger 165 Aylesbury and Leighton Buzzard (GR 659299).

THE WALK

1. Head along the tarmac footpath down the left-hand side of the pub and this takes you out onto Main Street by the church. Go left up the road a few yards then cross over by the nursery school and down School Lane. Pass by the right side of the white bungalow and through

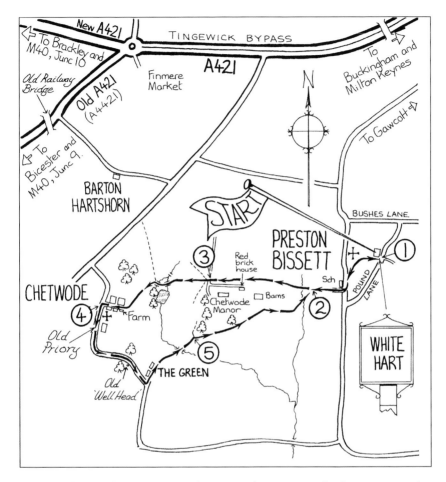

the gate beyond. Carry on in the same direction as the lane, across the field and up to the next gate.

2. On the other side of the gate continue straight ahead towards the red-brick house on the horizon. This takes you over a small bridge and up to a stile and gate in the top right corner of the field. Go over this, up the right-hand side of the field beyond and then over the stile at the top. Across the other side of this next field is the aforementioned red-brick house and to its right a track and then a clump of small trees. You need to cross the field in roughly the same direction as before but head towards the right-hand end of the clump of trees, and then along the side of them up to the next hedge. Go through the silver gate in the hedge (ignore the one on your left) and walk parallel to the fenced

33

track with views of Chetwode Manor behind it. The low bank and ditch in this field could be an old moat or even the site of the long disappeared church of St Michael! Over the gate in the corner by the poplar, cross the road and then go through the two white gates beyond.

3. Cross straight over the next field and down to the group of poplars at the bottom. In the middle of these trees is a small plank bridge which you cross and then go through some scrub and over another bridge and stile beyond. In this next field turn left and head towards the farm, past the oak trees and up to the gap between the breeze block building and the longer stone one to its right. Go through the gate, past the farmhouse and up to the road.

4. Turn left and continue along the road for the next ½ mile, passing the Old Chetwode Priory and church, round a corner and then down to a clump of trees in a slight dip. Just off the right-hand side of the road here is a small well head which reads 'Praise God from whom all blessings flow' and is dated 1868. More than a century on, the water still flows although I would not recommend tasting it!

Carry on up the road to a sharp right bend where you turn left down the bridleway and past the cottages called The Green. Keep to the rough track as it bends down to a small stream and then up the other side along the hedge on your left.

5. After 100 yards the track turns left through a gap in the hedge but you fork right, across the field towards the clump of trees on the top of the ridge. From here you can see the south front of Chetwode Manor, passed earlier, which dates back to around 1600. Go to the right of the clump of trees (which surrounds a pond) and then carry on towards the corner of the field where you will find a stile and bridge. Cross these and go along the left side of the field beyond until just before the fence at the bottom there is a gate and then a stile. Once over the stile head across the next field in the direction of the poplars by the white house on the horizon. This will take you up to the gate at point 2 on the outward walk, and you can follow the same route back into the village and to the White Hart.

Steeple Claydon
The Phoenix

This walk links all that is best in the villages of Steeple and Middle Claydon and takes you right up to the front door of Claydon House. There are picture postcard cottages, grand houses, avenues of oaks and pleasant views over lakes and fields.

Steeple Claydon is one of four Claydon villages and is not surprisingly the one with the steeple! All four villages have come under the influence of the Verney family who have owned Claydon House for nearly 400 years. The Second Earl set about rebuilding the house in the mid 18th century to better the home of one of his political rivals at Stowe, but financial ruin left only part of the work completed. Despite this the magnificent state rooms and the famous Chinese Room make it worth a visit. Florence Nightingale was the sister of Lady Verney and once occupied rooms here which now house a museum dedicated to her. It is said that some of the tall cedar trees around the house have grown from seeds she brought back from the Crimea! Between Easter and the end of October the house is open to the public from 1 pm to

5 pm on Saturday to Wednesday. Telephone: 01296 730349.

The Phoenix is one of a line of pretty houses and cottages which stand on the highest point of the village near the church. The main body of the pub is a black and white timber-framed building which has been here even longer than the Verneys. Its trim thatched roof has tiny dormer windows peeking out from under its rim. Inside there is a tidy saloon bar to your left with pool table and stone fireplace while to your right is the lounge bar. This opens out to an additional large family room making this a deceptively spacious pub. Behind the bar you will find handpumps dispensing Tetley, 6X and a guest beer while there is also a selection of wines and spirits. Griddled steak, chicken and salmon top the menu with home-made sausages, omelettes, scampi and vegetarian pasta being some of the alternatives. There is also a selection of baguettes, sandwiches and sweets.

The highlight of this pub to me is the massive garden. An old picture over the bar shows that it was previously used as a vegetable plot and orchard. Some of those trees remain but the rest is grass and flower beds with numerous tables and a small patio area. You can access the garden from round the right-hand side of the building. The opening hours are 12 noon to 3 pm and 6 pm to 11 pm on Monday to Thursday, 12 noon to 11 pm on Friday and Saturday and 12 noon to 10.30 pm on Sunday. Food is served from 12 noon to 8.30 pm on Friday and Saturday, 12 noon to 7 pm on Sunday and 12 noon to 2.30 pm and in the evenings on Monday to Thursday. The Phoenix is one of those rare pubs which has adapted to modern demands for food and the family without losing its local feel.

Telephone: 01296 738919.

- **HOW TO GET THERE:** From Buckingham head down the A413 towards Aylesbury and after a few miles and a long straight the road goes uphill and enters Padbury. On top of the hill and just before the garage turn right and follow this road through the village, round a left bend and then on for a few miles until it ends at a T junction in Steeple Claydon. Turn right and the Phoenix is immediately on your left.
- **PARKING:** There are a few spaces at the front of the pub but also plenty of room along the road.
- **LENGTH OF THE WALK:** 3 miles. Maps: OS Explorer 192 Buckingham and Milton Keynes or Landranger 165 Aylesbury and Leighton Buzzard (GR 701268).

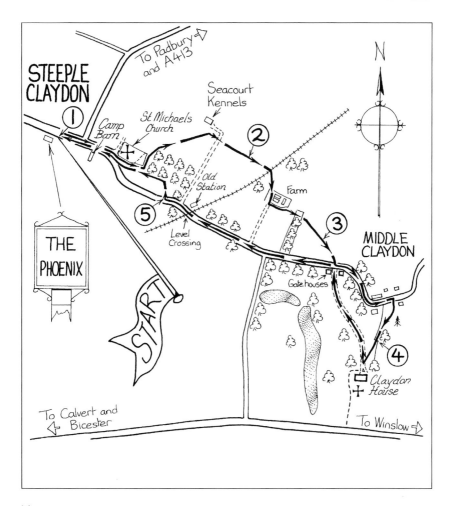

THE WALK

1. With your back to the pub turn right and walk along the pavement on the left-hand side of the road. On the right just past the Padbury turning is Camp Barn with a plaque set in its wall. It reads 'Around this spot, the Army of the Parliament under the command of Cromwell was encamped March 1644. And in the 3rd of the month advanced from here to the attack on Hillesden House'. Carry on up to the church where to the right of its entrance is a footpath sign and gate. Pass through this and walk along the edge of the churchyard (the footpath actually crosses the graveyard but I prefer to go around the outside). At the end of the fence turn left and walk along the rear of the churchyard

Middle Claydon

and then, turning slightly right, walk across to the stile in the fence on the other side of the avenue of oaks.

Go over the stile and cross the field diagonally towards the right of the red-brick house on the other side (Seacourt Kennels). As you approach the far corner you will see a gap in the hedge on your right with a stile and plank bridge. Go over these and across the track on the other side where you will find a piece of fence with two direction arrows on it. Take the right-hand path which goes straight across the field up to another stile.

2. Go over the stile and carry on in the same direction up to the railway which you cross by the stiles. In the next field turn 30 degrees to your right and head towards the right-hand end of the farm buildings. Go through the gateposts, walk past the ends of the buildings and start down the straight track ahead. But just as you leave the farm and cross a rather muddy cattle grid turn left and walk along the top of the field past the farmhouse and towards the trees where you will find a stile about 40 yards down from the corner of the field. Go across this stile, pass through the trees and over the stile on the other side, then turn 20 degrees right and head towards the white gatehouses in the distance.

3. Over the next stile is another avenue of oaks which you cross, then carry on to the gate in the hedge which puts you on the road in front of the gatehouses. Turn left and walk up the road, round a right bend, a left bend and then along the straight road past the trim brick houses and cottages of Middle Claydon. These are 18th and 19th-century, built as part of the Verney Estate. Halfway down this straight and just past the post box on your right is a footpath sign and gate. Go through this and, turning to your right, head towards Claydon House the end of which you can see through the trees. Halfway to it there is an oak tree and just beyond it in the fence on the right is a gate set at right angles.

4. Go through the gate and walk up to the front of the house. You can go right at the front gate and walk along the footpath which goes around the right-hand side of the house to the church behind it. There are also some permissive paths through the parkland if time allows.

From the front of the house turn back and walk along the driveway with views over the lakes on your left. Go through the gatehouses, turn left and walk along the road back towards Steeple Claydon. Ignore the left-hand turn and carry on over the railway and then along the pavement on the right-hand side.

5. The pavement ends at a gate in the hedge which you pass through and then, turning left, walk along the line of oaks back past the churchyard and onto the road by St Michael's. Carry on along the road to return to the Phoenix.

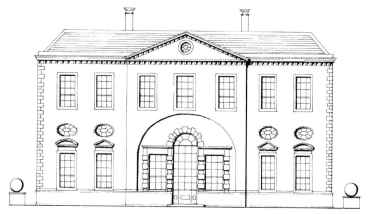

Claydon House (west front)

⑧ Wing
The Cock Inn

The advantage of this figure of eight walk is that you can do the short loop, the longer loop or both, depending on time and energy! The southern part takes you past Ascott House and through the deserted garden terraces of its predecessor. The northerly route passes over rolling countryside and visits the pretty hamlet of Burcott. In the middle is the village of Wing with its ancient church and old castle mound.

This historic village was until recently under threat from the proposed third London airport. Perhaps someone thought a place called Wing would be an appropriate site for aeroplanes; the locals did not agree and the plans were abolished, leaving the peaceful countryside for us to enjoy.

Wing has the oldest building in the county in the form of All Saints' church. The tall nave is nearly 1,200 years old while the seven-sided apse with the crypt below is one of only four left in the country. The village was of great importance in Saxon times and although this later waned a Norman castle was still built here, the mound of which stands at the top of the High Street. Ascott House is another reason to visit Wing. This National Trust property was an old timber-framed farmhouse which the Rothschilds (see Walk 10) extended in the 1870s. Its gardens are of equal note and well worth visiting when open (telephone: 01296 688242).

The Cock Inn is another North Bucks hostelry which hides its treasures behind a plain façade. As soon as you drive into the massive car park at the back, the pub's true heritage is exposed with rambling roofs, and timber frames infilled with red brick. The main entrance is from the rear and this leads you into either the restaurant area on your left or the main bar on your right. The entire interior has recently been renovated, enhancing the rustic aura, but your eyes will probably be first drawn to the huge bars! An army of handpumps dispense Webster's and Directors among others, and as you would expect there is a good selection of wines and spirits. You are spoilt when it comes to food. There are bar snacks from sandwiches and ploughman's to cooked meals or you can eat from the buffet in the restaurant area next door. This is an impressive, well thought out enterprise which is well staffed and, with baby changing rooms and a garden with kiddies' play area, a pub for all the family. The opening times are 11.30 am to 3 pm and 6 pm to 11 pm on Monday to Saturday; 12 noon to 3 pm and 7 pm to 10.30 pm on Sunday.

Telephone: 01296 688214.

- **HOW TO GET THERE:** From Aylesbury take the A418 to Leighton Buzzard and after about 8 miles you enter Wing. The main road takes a sharp left turn then as it is about to go right you turn off onto the road to Stewkley (in effect straight on) and a hundred yards up here on the right you will find the Cock Inn. From Milton Keynes follow the route described to the Three Locks (Walk 5) but carry on all the way into Linslade. At the traffic lights before the canal bridge turn right up the A418 to Aylesbury and after 3 miles you enter Wing. As the road makes a sharp left turn you go right up the road to Stewkley and you will find the pub on the right.
- **PARKING:** There is a large car park behind the pub, but you can usually find plenty of spaces along the road.
- **LENGTH OF THE WALK:** 4 miles in total, made up of a loop of 2$\frac{1}{2}$ miles and one of 1$\frac{1}{2}$ miles. Maps: OS Explorer 192 Buckingham and Milton Keynes or Landranger 165 Aylesbury and Leighton Buzzard (GR 882226).

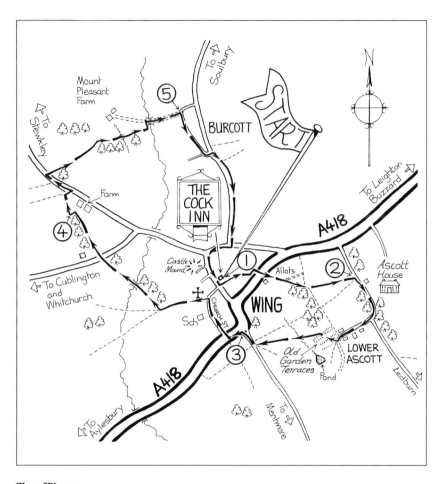

THE WALK

1. From the front of the Cock Inn turn left down Prospect Place, a short cul-de-sac which runs down the side of the pub. At the end continue down the footpath, between the houses and onto the main road. Turn left along the pavement for a few yards and cross the road by the bollards, over to the Sports and Social Club. Just to the left of this is a gate and stile leading into the allotments which you cross. Follow the path along the right-hand side of the allotments and then as it turns left and cuts across the middle, carry straight on down a vague path, along the hedge with tall trees and into the corner. Cross the stile and take the left-hand path which leaves the hedge and cuts straight over the field.

    2. Go through the hedge on the other side and onto the road. Turn

All Saints' church, Wing

right and walk down the quiet lane past the side entrance to Ascott House, through a tree tunnel and round a sharp right bend. Turn right here (in effect straight on) and walk through Lower Ascott until the road ends at a gate. Go round this and along the concrete track for a few yards until you reach a stile in the fence on the right. Once over this you take the right-hand path in the direction of the sign which leads you up the terraces and through the gap in the banks at the top. These are the remains of the 17th-century gardens of the lost Ascott House. This belonged to the Dormers who have a huge monument in Wing church. If you stood at the top and looked down the terraces nearly 400 years ago you would have seen beautiful flower beds, lawns, trees and a landscaped park.

From the top turn slightly to your left and head down to the stile, over the muddy stream and up the other side to the large tree in the top corner. Go right along the road which returns you to the corner of the A418.

3. Turn left along the road then cross over by the first right turn which is Church Street. Walk down this back road until at a sharp right turn there is the entrance to the church. The walk continues along the tarmac path to your left between the line of yews and the hedge, but if you have the time take a look at All Saints' church. The path leads you to the back of the churchyard then through a kissing gate, across the next field and down to a stile and bridge in the hedge. Over these turn right (ignoring the other two routes offered) and walk along the hedge on your right, over a bridge and up the other side until you reach a road. Cross this, go over the stile on the other side and then walk up the left-hand side of the field. As you come alongside the farm on your right you reach the top of the field. Go through the gate in the left corner and in the field beyond you will see a gap in the hedge on the right about 30 yards away.

4. Go through this gap and walk up the left-hand side of the next field to the stile at the top. Over this turn right and cross over the gate onto the road. Turn left and walk along the roadside, into a dip where you cross over and head down the bridleway on the other side. This takes you along the right of a large field until at the bottom you go through the gap in the hedge. Continue along the path with the wire fence on your left and a marshy area with white poplars on your right. This eventually takes you down between the trees, over a small ditch and along the right-hand side of the field beyond. At the end you turn left and reach the driveway to Mount Pleasant Farm.

Turn right, over the bridge and up the drive to the road at the top.

5. Turn right and walk down the road through the pretty cottages of Burcott. This leads you up to Soulbury Road opposite a telephone box. Cross over here, turn right and walk along the pavement all the way back into Wing. At the T junction at the top of the hill turn right and follow the road round a sharp left bend, past the old castle mound on your right and back to the Cock Inn.

Marsh Gibbon
The Plough

In contrast to the Chilterns to the south this route leads you through flat, rich pasture intersected by numerous streams and ponds. As a result you only have to make a short climb to take advantage of some spectacular views. Also of note is the wide variety of animals and birds you can see close at hand.

This rather odd village name has quite a straightforward origin; as soon as you walk off the slight rising it is built on, you enter wet, boggy fields, while the latter part of the name is that of the family who owned the manor in the 13th century. The present Manor House, opposite the Plough, is a hotchpotch but is still a grand looking building, constructed of local stone in Elizabethan times. This limestone, found only in the far reaches of the county, gives the village a Cotswold feel and was still in use when Sir Henry Acland built the row of semi-detached estate cottages you see on your right, just before the village pond. These date from the 1880s and came after Sir Henry had greatly improved the state of what was then a run down village. The locals had always been able to look after themselves though as in 1788 they founded The Greyhound Club. This was a Friendly Society (forerunners to modern day insurance companies) and was named after the pub of the same name. The Society and pub still survive today but most of the once numerous 'watering holes' have gone (look out for house names like The Old Red Lion).

The Plough is a pleasant exception to this rule. It is a 16th-century coaching inn with a limestone exterior and casement windows although there is no sign of the original archway for coaches. An impressive fluted chimney stack leads down to a large inglenook fire which is the dominant feature as you enter the lounge bar. The beamed ceiling maintains the antiquated feel and the simple decor prevents it becoming too twee. The wide selection of wines and malt whiskies catches the eye behind the bar while in addition to the traditional pub fare, there are meals for vegetarians, children and lovers of the humble sandwich. The Sunday roast is a highlight.

The pubs tend to be large in many North Bucks villages, and this is no exception. There is plenty of parking, a garden at the rear and also a separate restaurant. Opening times are 12 noon to 2.30 pm and 6 pm to 11 pm (no food on Mondays or on Sunday evenings).

Telephone: 01869 277305.

- **HOW TO GET THERE:** From Aylesbury take the A41 towards Bicester and after about 13 miles and literally just before the low railway bridge turn right to Marsh Gibbon. Upon entering the village the road twists left then right, past a pond and then opposite the left turn to Poundon you reach the Plough.
- **PARKING:** There is a car park behind the pub but also plenty of space along the road.
- **LENGTH OF THE WALK:** 3^1/$_2$ miles. Maps: OS Explorer 192 Buckingham and Milton Keynes or Landranger 165 Aylesbury and Leighton Buzzard (GR 647231).

THE WALK

1. From the Plough head along Church Street towards Bicester, using the pavement on the right-hand side. This takes you past attractive stone and timber cottages. Just before the pond take the right turn to Bicester, go past the bus shelter and then turn right down Ware Leys Close (by the footpath sign). This road quickly ends and turns into a muddy track up the left side of house No. 2 which stops at a gate. Go through this and cross straight over the field beyond to the gates opposite. In the next field walk around the right-hand side which after a left turn follows a small stream and hedge up to the top corner.

2. Cross straight over the stile in front with an arrow on it telling you that you have joined the Cross Bucks Way. Walk up the left-hand side of the field past the barns on your left and over the hedge in front. Go diagonally across the next field in the direction of the arrow (towards the right of the red house on the horizon) then over a plank bridge and stile in the hedge on the other side. Now walk to the stile in the hedge just past the left-hand end of the line of conifers, and then in the next field go up to the right side of the clump of trees ahead. Go past the arrow on a post and up to the fence where you go left, then immediately right and down the steps to the railway line. Walk up the other side and continue up the next field where, as you reach the top of the hill, a red-brick shed appears on your left. About 100 yards past it in the hedge is a stile with a splendid view across to Poundon House. This is, unusually for Buckinghamshire, built of ironstone and is only about 90 years old!

3. Cross the stile and turn right; follow the hedge along the top of the ridge, then walk round the pond and up to the stile ahead. Turn slightly left across the next field to the right of a small clump of trees and go over the stile there. Walk up the left of the field beyond for 100 yards and then by the stile in the hedge turn right across the same field and continue through the gate on the other side. Go over the road and along the right-hand side of the field beyond which curves round to a gap in the next hedge.

4. Carry on along the right side of the field (although if it doesn't damage the crop you can go straight over the top of the hill) and at the bottom turn left until on your right you find a plank bridge and stile. Go over this and, turning slightly right, cross to the stile beyond. This puts you back on the railway where you turn left along the track for 20 yards and then right up the other side. Go over another stile and then along the trees on your right. Pass a pond and then turn sharp right at the end of the hedge. (If you have surplus energy then you could carry on up Windmill Hill beyond with excellent views.) Follow the hedge to the bottom of the field and the next stile.

5. From here the route back to the village has few features to guide you. Rely on the arrows as their directions are accurate. Cross the field in front up to the stile in the ragged hedge beyond, then bear slightly right in the next field to the bridge over the straight stream. Turn left in

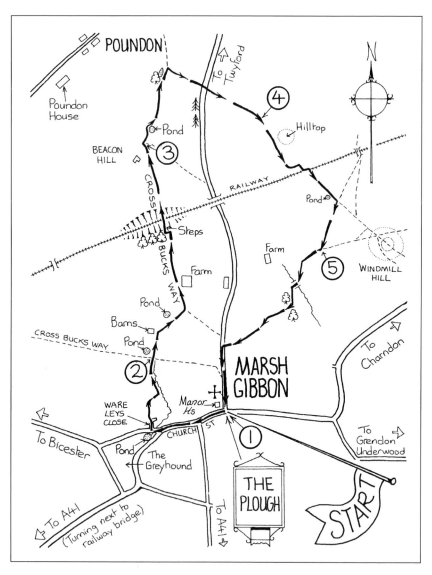

the next field over to the trees where you need to keep a sharp eye out for the stile at the junction of three hedges. Over the stile you turn right along the top of the field then go over the stile in the far corner. Cross into the opposite corner of the next field and then again in the field beyond which takes you onto Station Road. Turn left into the village, past the church and Manor House and back to the Plough.

⑩ Waddesdon
The Five Arrows Hotel

This walk will take you from one Rothschild estate to another. From Waddesdon and the maroon-trimmed houses with their five arrows emblems to the top of Eythrope Park with its pastoral insignia. On the way you pass through woods, parkland and fields, and there are numerous dramatic views.

One day in 1877 the peace of the village of Waddesdon was shattered by the sounds of building on the previously bare Lodge Hill. Teams of workmen had invaded and started levelling off the top of the hill. Slowly over the next few years a grand house with an array of turrets and ornate chimneys rose to dominate the view until fully matured trees were dragged up and planted to mask it from the public's gaze.

The house was built for Baron Ferdinand de Rothschild so that he could be within easy reach of London, impress guests with his taste in architecture and go hunting for which the Vale was noted. Six of his relatives also bought estates in the area, including his sister who became his neighbour when she purchased Eythrope Park. They were all descended from the five sons of Mayer Amschel who had sent them to the European capitals of commerce, Frankfurt, Vienna, Naples, Paris and London to establish banks. The Rothschild family crest has five arrows on it to represent these brothers; hence the name of the hotel.

The Five Arrows Hotel was built in 1887 as part of the Waddesdon Estate and originally accommodated architects and craftsmen who were working on the Manor. The exterior is in a picturesque Old English style with mock timber framing, ornate chimneys and wrought ironwork (which is probably older than the building). Despite the rich exterior, the inside is surprisingly light and beautifully decorated with period wallpaper and furniture.

Behind the bar you will find Adnams and London Pride on handpump and an impressive collection of wines, including some from the Rothschild vineyards. High quality food, though, is the highlight of your visit. A mouthwatering mix of English and Mediterranean cuisine is always on offer, with such delights as Dover sole grilled on the bone, chargrilled aubergines and a selection of Italian meats with melon, figs and olives. Vegetarians are catered for and children are welcome, with highchairs and booster seats available. There is a lunchtime snack menu from Monday to Saturday and the ornate gardens and terrace give further space for eating and drinking outside. The opening times are 11 am to 3 pm and 6 pm to 11 pm on Monday to Saturday and 12 noon to 3 pm and 7 pm to 10.30 pm on Sunday (NB: there is no lunchtime snack menu on a Sunday). Telephone: 01296 651727.

Waddesdon Manor (NT) is open from the beginning of April to the end of October on Thursday to Sunday, 11 am to 4 pm (last admissions to house 2.30 pm). It is also open on bank holidays and on Wednesdays in July and August. The grounds are open for a greater part of the year. Tickets to the house are sold on a first come, first served basis but are bookable. For full information telephone: 01296 651211.

- **HOW TO GET THERE:** Waddesdon is on the A41 between Aylesbury and Bicester. The Five Arrows Hotel is in the middle of the village next to the entrance to the Manor.
- **PARKING:** There are a few spaces at the front of the Five Arrows but there is usually plenty of room along the main road.
- **LENGTH OF THE WALK:** $4\frac{1}{2}$ miles. Maps: OS Explorer 181 (formerly 2) Chiltern Hills North or Landranger 165 Aylesbury and Leighton Buzzard (GR 741168).

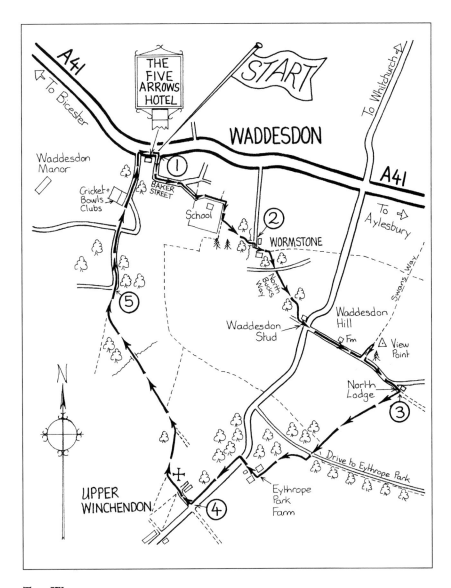

THE WALK

1. From the front of the Five Arrows Hotel head along the main road away from the entrance to the Manor and past the telephone box. Turn right down Baker Street and follow it round the left-hand bend and up to the fork where you go right down School Lane. At the school gates take the footpath to their left which takes you around its perimeter. The tarmac path turns off to the left before you reach the end of the sports field, but you carry on down between the fences and then right, still following the perimeter of the school. Halfway down this straight turn left over a stile and along the North Bucks Way (you follow this all the way to North Lodge). Cross the field then go through the wood, over a tiny stream and onto the road in front of an impressive 18th-century brick house.

2. Turn right and then left up the path marked for the Midshires and North Bucks Ways. As the path emerges from between the fences it forks and you follow the right-hand one between the trees which takes you over a tarmac drive and the fence beyond. Head up the left-hand side of the hedge in front of you which climbs up to the edge of a small plantation where you find a stile to cross. Carry on the ascent through the trees, over a clearing and then back through woodland until reaching a stile. From here you cross the field beyond diagonally to a point about 20 yards to the right of the barn where you go over another stile and follow the path beyond as it bends left and leads you along the front of Waddesdon Stud. At the end you cross the road (watch out for cars which can come hurtling around the bend!) and go up the tarmac lane on the other side. This leads you all the way to North Lodge but before you get there take a left turn at the top of the hill by the cedars, along Swans Way, and admire the views over the Vale.

3. You will recognise North Lodge by the three panels in the masonry with pastoral insignia and the Rothschilds' motto 'Concordia, Industria, Integritas'. In front of the house the tarmac road veers left but you go right down the side of the house and then at the gate turn right and follow the footpath which clings to the hedge along the top of the field. At the end of the field you pass between large trees which line the tarmac drive to Eythrope Park. Cross this and head between the copper beeches, slightly up the drive on the other side, where you will find a gap in the fence. Go through here and turn immediately right and follow the edge of the field all the way to Eythrope Park Farm. Pass the crumbling front of the farmhouse (probably faced with clunch, a hard layer of chalk, which is prone to deteriorate like this) and then turn right and along the track up to the main road.

Turn left and walk along the right-hand side of the road until, just past the Upper Winchendon sign, there is a crossroads of tracks.

4. Go down the right-hand one and then carry straight on through the gate as the track turns right behind Wilderness Barn. Walk down the hill alongside the fence on your right. The church behind the fence

View from Upper Winchendon

is about 800 years old. The undulations in the field and the old avenue you will shortly join are probably remains of the once extensive gardens of the manor house which pre-date Waddesdon Manor by about 150 years. Just before reaching the bottom there is a stile in the fence; turn right over it and head diagonally across the next field, aiming to the right of the line of trees. This takes you up a bank and onto a track, along which you turn left. This is the old avenue and you follow it down over the tiny stream and up the other side where, halfway up the hill, it bends to the right and takes you up to a gate.

5. Go through this gate and you are on a 90 degree bend in a road. Take the right-hand way (with glimpses of the manor house to your left) all the way down to a T junction where, ignoring the tarmac road, you carry straight on over the grass. This takes you past the Bowls and Cricket Clubs and then rejoins the road which you follow through the trees, past the main gate and back onto the A41 next to the Five Arrows Hotel.

⑪ Cheddington
The Old Swan

The Grand Union Canal forms the backbone of this walk with the popular village of Marsworth as the highlight. Its quaint cottages and church overlook the waterway which is usually lined with colourful narrowboats.

Cheddington's main claim to fame is the Great Train Robbery of 1963, when a post office train was held up near the station to the north. The village prior to this had serviced the nearby Mentmore House, a Rothschild mansion (see Walk 10) designed by Sir Joseph Paxton of Great Exhibition fame. A few Arts and Crafts style houses in the village were built for the estate workers in the 1870s. There are, though, some houses of even greater antiquity, such as the Old Swan.

This 17th-century hostelry, set back from the road, has an ample car park, children's play area and seating in the front garden with some old railway station scales and a porter's trolley as decoration. Overlooking this is the rambling timber-framed pub with painted brick infilling and a thatched roof. Richly coloured hanging baskets add the final touch to the delightful exterior.

On entering you can turn left into the country-style dining area with wallpaper, quarry tiles and pine furniture, while to your right is the main bar with oak floor, low ceiling and exposed beams. In the corner is an inglenook fireplace surrounded by brasses and to the right the rare sight these days of a piano! You can eat on either side, choosing from the wide range of food which includes vegetarian and children's meals as well as sandwiches, baked potatoes and puddings. Beers on handpump include Speckled Hen, Tetley and a local special like Notley or Ridgeway Bitter. There is also a selection of malts and wines. Best of all, this attractive stop is open all day: 11 am to 11 pm on Monday to Saturday and 12 noon to 10.30 pm on Sunday. Food is served from 12 noon to 2.30 pm and 7 pm to 9 pm on Monday to Friday and from 12 noon to 4 pm and 7 pm to 9.30 pm on Saturday and Sunday.

Telephone: 01296 668226.

- **HOW TO GET THERE:** From Aylesbury head towards Tring on the A41 and at the second roundabout in Aston Clinton (next to the Rising Sun) turn left up the B489 to Ivinghoe. Follow this road for the next few miles, through a number of left and right bends and over the canal at Marsworth. Just after this the road climbs over a hill and then drops down to cross the railway. Just before the bridge turn left down the road to Cheddington. This goes over a narrow canal bridge and then past the speed signs and into the village. The Old Swan is one of the first buildings on the left.
- **PARKING:** There is a car park to the front of the pub but alternative parking is available along the road or to the right as you enter the village, beside the tennis courts.
- **LENGTH OF THE WALK:** 4 miles (short cuts at Manor Farm or bridge 130 will knock off 1/2 mile or so). Maps: OS Explorer 181 Chiltern Hills North or Landranger 165 Aylesbury and Leighton Buzzard (GR 923170).

THE WALK

1. With your back to the pub turn right and walk along the pavement, then on the road out of the village (the left-hand side is better except around the left bend beside the house). After the bend the road straightens and halfway towards the canal bridge there is a road turning on the left. Go up here under the tall railway bridge and immediately after it turn right over a stile. Follow the path over another stile before crossing a narrow field up to a wire fence. You could simply turn right

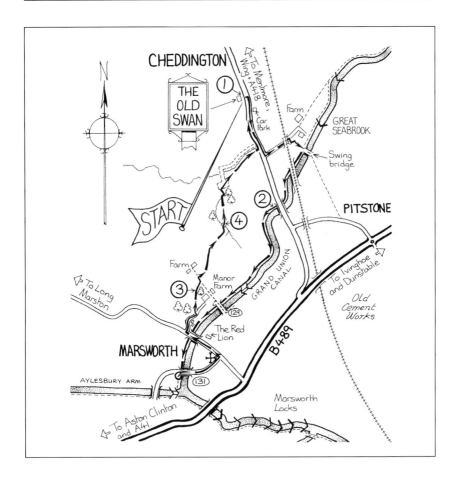

here and keep to the right-hand side of the fence up to the swing bridge. The official footpath is over the stile, turning right and continuing along the left-hand side of the fence but this involves climbing over a wire which the farmer has put across the path near the bridge! Whichever route you take, on reaching the swing bridge turn right and follow the canal under the main London-Birmingham railway, round a bend and then under the Cheddington road. (For a short history of the canal see Walk 5.)

2. You keep along the towpath on the right-hand side of the canal all the way to bridge 131. You will notice the white tinge to the water which comes from years of outfall from the nearby Pitstone Cement Works. This seems to have had no adverse effect on the wildlife

The Grand Union Canal

judging by the shoals of sizable carp basking in the sun when I walked here on a July day.

At bridge 131 pass under it then turn right up on to the road, then right again over the bridge and up the quiet lane to the T junction beside the church. Turn left down past the Red Lion, go over the canal and then turn right down the tarmac lane. This runs around the rear of two white cottages, through some trees and then up to the gate of Manor Farm in front of which you turn left. Go over the stile then head for the opposite corner of the field in the direction of the arrow to the next stile which lies under the furthest left of the tall poplar trees.

3. Go over this stile and on in the same direction to a strip of new fencing in the hedge on your left (beside some recently planted trees). Go over the stile here and turn immediately right along the hedge up to another stile. Over this turn 30 degrees left and cross the field to the opposite corner (in line with the right-hand end of the hill on the horizon). This will take you over the wire fences which divide this field and past what looks like an old dried-up moat on your left. In the top corner cross the stiles and bridge then, turning slightly right, go down the middle of a strip of grassland between the fence and hedge. In summer this is full of a wide variety of butterflies and birds. At the end cross the stile and walk along the hedge then turn left up to a bridge with a metal rail.

4. Over the bridge turn 45 degrees left and cross the field towards the tall trees and the hill behind. Just before the trees there is a post where you turn slightly right up to the trees then bend left along them and up to the top of the field. Go over the stile in this corner and across the concrete area in the direction of the arrow up to a stile on the far side. Cross this and continue along in the direction of the railway bridge on the horizon which leads you up to join and walk along the right-hand side of a hedge. This follows a small ditch up to a spring on the other side of the road. This is the infant River Thame which passes through Aylesbury and Thame before joining its namesake the Thames. At the end you reach the Cheddington Road where you turn left and follow it back to the Old Swan.

12 Dinton
The Seven Stars

A walk from one dispersed set of pretty cottages and houses to another, with crop fields in between. Views over the Vale to the distant grey ridge of the Chilterns are frequent despite the low setting of the route. There is the added bonus of another excellent pub halfway round, named after the famous Dinton Hermit.

Set in a little dip just off the main Aylesbury to Thame road, Dinton bears more than a passing resemblance to an idyllic Devon village. This is due to the use of 'witchert', a mix of mud and straw used to build walls just as cob is used in the South West. As it is not waterproof the walls are set on a base of stones, with whitewashed sides and a thatched or tiled roof. These characteristic cottages line the pretty winding High Street which leads up to Dinton Hall, once the home of Simon Mayne. He was one of the Puritans who signed the death warrant of Charles I, only to meet his maker in the Tower some years later. His servant John Biggs was so distressed that he wandered the local area and became known as the Dinton Hermit.

Hidden in the trees by the main crossroads on the A418 is Dinton Folly or Castle. It was built in 1769 for Sir John Vanhattem as an eyecatcher from his house and it has within its walls fossil ammonites from his personal collection.

The Seven Stars is attractively set and an immaculately kept lawn surrounds the rambling white building. Inside, the pleasant lounge bar with beamed ceiling leads round to 'the snug' with its famous ancient settles and large inglenook fireplace. Edgars and ABC are on handpump and there is a selection of wines and spirits. The excellent menu caters for all tastes and specialities include 'Surf and Turf' (steak and scampi), carbonnade of beef, four different steak and fish dishes and a separate vegetarian selection. There are also sandwiches, ploughman's, salads and jacket potatoes. (On Sundays only these snack choices are available, along with a roast.) The opening times are 12 noon to 3 pm and 6 pm to 11 pm on Monday to Saturday (closed on Tuesday evening) and 12 noon to 3 pm and 7 pm to 10.30 pm on Sunday.

Telephone: 01296 748241.

- **HOW TO GET THERE:** From Aylesbury take the A418 towards Thame, going through the village of Stone and out the other side. Carry on over the crossroads by the Folly, ignoring the left turn to Dinton, but take the next left after this opposite the bus shelter. Continue down New Road, enter the village and you will find the Seven Stars on the left just before the T junction.
- **PARKING:** There is a car park at the side of the pub and ample parking along the road.
- **LENGTH OF THE WALK:** 3½ miles. Maps: OS Explorer 181 (formerly 2) Chiltern Hills North or Landranger 165 Aylesbury and Leighton Buzzard (GR 763107).

THE WALK

1. Start by heading down the tarmac lane from the pub car park, past the front of the Seven Stars and down to the corner of the road. Go left here which leads you round a sharp left then right-hand bend (use the pavement on the right-hand side) and carry on up the road all the way up to the church. Go through the church gate and follow the path round the right of the tower. Take a moment to look in the porch and notice the elaborate carving around the church door. It's very rare and more than 800 years old. Carry on under the yews, out onto a small

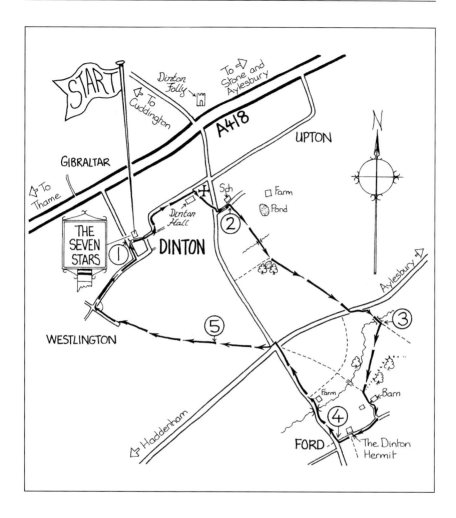

green and head down towards School Lane on the opposite side. Notice the two timber-framed cottages that mirror each other. These were once one large house which has had the middle knocked through!

2. Turn left down School Lane and then in front of the school go right and over the stile signposted for the Aylesbury Ring. (You now follow the Aylesbury Ring all the way to the Dinton Hermit.) The direction of the sign is fairly accurate and leads you across the field to the left-hand end of the nearest hedge in front of you (towards a dip in the distant Chiltern Hills) and then along the hedge behind it. At the bottom cross the fence and small bridge and carry on across the next field to the stile at the left-hand end of the clump of trees. Go over this and turn slightly to your left and cross the field diagonally. At the next stile turn slightly right and head towards the corner at the end of the tall hedge on your left. This puts you onto what can be a busy road, so cross over carefully, turn left and walk along the verge until you reach a gate and stile on your right and another Aylesbury Ring sign. Cross the stile, turn left 30 to 40 degrees and walk towards the small bridge in the hedge in front.

3. Once over the bridge the path forks and you take the right-hand one across the field which narrows with a hedge on your left and the stream on your right. At the end there is a gate in the left corner which you pass through and then, turning slightly left, head between the barn and bungalow. You cross another stile and then follow the concrete drive from the barn down to the road. Turn right on the road and follow it past the Dinton Hermit (or not, if you require refreshment) and up to the main road.

4. Turn right and keep to this side of the road over the bridge, past the farm and on up to the crossroads. In the opposite corner is a footpath sign and gap in the hedge. Cross the roads and go through here and across the field beyond in the direction of the sign. Go over the next stile and the field beyond to the gap in the hedge where there is another stile to pass over.

5. Cross the field beyond by heading for the top left corner. You can get a glimpse of the illusive Dinton Hall through the trees on your right. In the corner go over the stile and walk along the hedge on your left up to the top of this last field where you cross onto the end of a road. Go right up this lane to the crossroads on the small green and turn right. This is Westlington whose name is a corruption of West Dinton. Go past La Chouette restaurant and follow this road until the next left turn which takes you up a slight hill and back to the Seven Stars.

⒀ Ickford
The Rising Sun

Lovely throughout the year, meadows of lush grass and buttercups watered by the River Thame make this a particularly memorable walk on a lazy summer's day. The ridges and furrows in many of the fields are remains of medieval farming and show that this landscape has been unchanged for centuries. The rustic churches and timber-framed cottages maintain this antique aura.

Ickford is a long village set parallel to the River Thame with two picturesque bridges of great antiquity. The medieval stone bridge is probably 600 years old and replaced a wooden one which was known to have been standing in 1237. The second, smaller bridge crosses The Whirlpool, so named as the bottom of the silent pond has never been found! Ickford's greatest claim to fame is Gilbert Sheldon who was rector here until 1660 when he was called to London and in 1663 became the Archbishop of Canterbury. The main road which links both ends of the village bears his name. The great charm of the village is in its houses and cottages, none more quaint than the Rising Sun.

This pretty black and white building dates back to the 17th century and still retains its thatched roof which rolls down over tiny dormer windows. On entering you are welcomed by a low ceiling and original beams with the bar standing opposite the large fireplace. To your left is a separate dining area with tapestry covered chairs while a scattering of wooden tables furnishes the main area.

Behind the bar you will find handpumps dispensing Pedigree, Hancock's and 6X, alongside a variety of wines, spirits and cider. The food includes rump steaks, cod, scampi, pies, sandwiches, vegetarian meals and a bargain Sunday roast! There is even a special blackboard for the selection of crisps! Another great feature is the garden which can be accessed from the car park or from inside the pub through the door marked 'Gentlemen'! It is huge, with benches, trees and a large play area set in bark chippings. This friendly pub is a must to visit. The opening hours are from 12 noon to 3 pm and 6 pm to 11 pm on Monday to Friday, 11 am to 11 pm on Saturday and 11 am to 10.30 pm on Sunday.

Telephone: 01844 339238.

- **HOW TO GET THERE:** From the M40, junction 8A, take the A418 towards Thame. After a few miles you enter Tiddington whereupon you turn left to Ickford (just beyond the garage and the Fox pub). After a mile or so you cross two narrow bridges and then enter the village. At the T junction turn left and follow the road round a right bend and after a few hundred yards you will find the Rising Sun.
- **PARKING:** There is a large car park to the side of the pub and ample space along the roadside.
- **LENGTH OF THE WALK:** 3$^1/_2$ miles. Maps: OS Explorer 180 Oxford, Witney and Woodstock or Landranger 164 Oxford and surrounding area (GR 649075).

THE WALK

1. With your back to the Rising Sun turn left and head back into the village along Worminghall Road. At the sharp left bend turn down Church Road, walk to the very end and visit St Nicholas's church. This Norman church has avoided destructive restoration and its interior is especially atmospheric. Go in and try and find the frame for Nine Men's Morris, an ancient game known to Shakespeare, which has been scratched into the windowsill of the north triple window.

From here go back 20 to 30 yards and turn right down the short drive

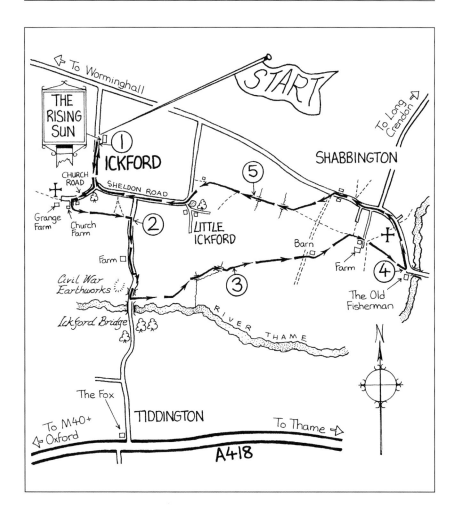

to Church Farm where a footpath leads off to the left of its gate. Follow this along the rear of the village, over a stile and straight across the field to the willow at the left-hand end of three new houses. Here you will find a fenced path taking you onto Bridge Road whereupon you turn right and follow it out of the village.

2. Keep to the right-hand side until after Whirlpool Farm where you should cross before going around the right-hand bend. Walk over the first bridge, then turn left over the stile (and a second shortly after) and walk parallel to the River Thame up to the next fence. Cross this stile and turning 30 degrees to your left cross the field (to the left-hand end

65

of the houses you can see on the horizon). This will take you up to a plank bridge in the hedge which you cross before carrying on along the right-hand side of the next field. In the corner you will find a more substantial bridge which leads you to another field. Turn 30 degrees left again and cross the field to come to a kissing gate.

3. Through the gate you carry on in roughly the same direction through another hedge and then towards a low tiled barn alongside the next hedge. Pass through this just to the right of the barn and turn 60 degrees left and cross the next field to its top right corner (towards the houses). Just before the corner there are two lowered posts in the fence on your right and a stile between them. Cross this and head for the next stile to the left of the bungalow. Go over this and along the right-hand side of the field onto the tarmac drive to Franklins Farm. Cross this slightly to your right and opposite the front of the bungalow is a stile with three direction arrows. Take the middle one and aim for the pub sign next to the lone building by the river. Note the ridges in this field, which are the remains of the medieval village, and the huge buttresses supporting the unstable tower of Shabbington church.

4. At the bottom cross the stiles and turn left along the pavement into the village (or take a halfway stop at the Old Fisherman). Follow the road through the village as it bends slowly left back to Ickford. As the road drops out of Shabbington there are two final houses either side of the road (just before the national speed limit signs). Go through the gate immediately after the left-hand one and rather than following the track turn 45 degrees and cross the field diagonally to a gap in the hedge. Here another path joins from the left and you cross the next short field roughly in its direction to a gate and bridge. Beyond these go straight across the field to another stile and an awkward plank bridge.

5. Walk along the hedge on the right-hand side of the next field and the one beyond up to its right-hand corner. Go over the stile here and in the same direction cross the field towards the corrugated shed. Just before reaching it turn 45 degrees left and head for the footpath sign and gate which puts you back on the road at Little Ickford, an idyllic spot with a pond surrounded by trees and cottages. From here head back into the village along Sheldon Road (notice the spiral chimney on St Julian Cottage) and round the right-hand bend to return to the Rising Sun.

Weston Turville
The Chequers

This is a short, easy to walk but very pretty stroll through the hidden parts of Weston Turville. It crosses untouched fields to Halton with its charming Rothschild cottages and then returns along the picturesque Wendover Arm of the Grand Union Canal. The final few hundred yards past the church are a real gem!

Behind the undistinguished façade that Weston Turville presents along the main road, winding lanes, timber-framed cottages and a tiny tree-lined stream are there to be discovered. The original settlement grew up where the manor and church are today and finds in this area date back to the Bronze Age. There is a good chance that there was a Roman villa here and there are remains of a large motte and bailey castle behind the Manor House. In the past few centuries the bulk of the village has formed along the Aston Clinton road leaving the old part as a tranquil oasis.

In the heart of this area is the Chequers, a cream-painted brick building which externally dates back a couple of hundred years. The adjoining barn has been converted into a restaurant and in the centre of the L-shape the buildings create is a patio packed with tables and chairs. Entering the pub through the porch leads you into the saloon bar with flagstone floor, exposed brick and flint walls and beamed ceiling. The rustic feel is enhanced by the fireplace to your right and the old timbers to the left. Behind the bar you will find handpumps with 6X, Adnams, London Pride and Wychert, while there is an excellent selection of wines and malts. The bar menu on blackboards above is comprehensive and includes a large selection of fish dishes, as well as sandwiches, ploughman's and vegetarian meals. If you want something more substantial then there is the quality restaurant next door. Although hidden at the back of the village this pub is justly renowned for its cuisine and for serving a good pint. The opening hours are 11.30 am to 3 pm and 6 pm to 11 pm (10.30 pm on Sunday); closed Monday lunchtime.

Telephone 01296 613298.

- **HOW TO GET THERE:** From Aylesbury head south along the A413 towards Wendover. Just past Stoke Mandeville turn left to Weston Turville. On entering the village go right opposite the Chandos Arms and then second left down School Lane. At the end turn left along Church Lane and you will shortly come across the Chequers.
- **PARKING:** There is a large car park to the rear of the pub or you can park along the road near the junction of Bates Lane and Church Lane.
- **LENGTH OF THE WALK:** 2½ miles. Maps: OS Explorer 181 (formerly 2) Chiltern Hills North or Landranger 165 Aylesbury and Leighton Buzzard (GR 858106).

THE WALK

1. With your back to the pub turn left and walk up Church Lane, past the junction with Bates Lane and then just past the brick and timber cottage (and as the modern houses start) turn right down the footpath. This takes you over the stream and up to a stile (beside a very attractive landscaped garden). Take the left hand of the two paths offered which takes you diagonally across the field in the direction of the left-hand end of the distant Chiltern Hills. Go over the next stile and onwards in the same direction past the right-hand side of tall trees and up to the next hedge.

2. Cross the stile and go to the white post in the next hedge (towards the left-hand end of the aircraft hangars). Over this, the next stile to

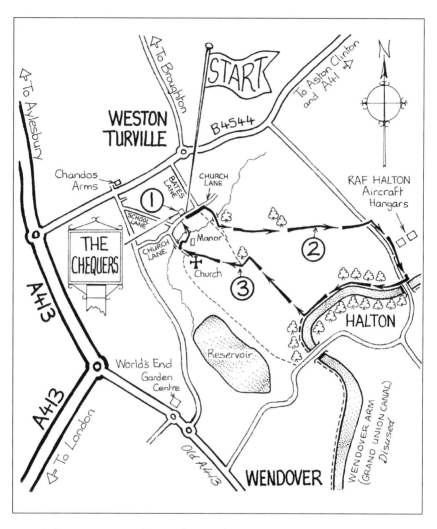

your left puts you on the road to Halton. Cross over and turn right and walk along the left-hand side which, when past RAF Halton, becomes a pavement. As you enter the village notice the plaster panels on some of the houses. These represent pastoral scenes and were built as part of the Rothschilds' Halton estate (see Walk 10). Alfred de Rothschild used to go around the estate in a carriage pulled by zebras and had his own private zoo!

When you reach the low bridge over the Wendover Arm of the Grand Union Canal, turn right and walk beside the canal, to the left of

A timber-framed cottage in Weston Turville

the white house and into the trees beyond. This pretty wooded stretch of water is made up of ash, oak, sycamore, maple and horse chestnut and is patrolled by moorhens. I even spotted a turtle, not an escapee from 'Mr Alfred's Zoo' but probably a discarded pet!

At the end of the long straight with views to your right across the Vale, and as the canal starts to bend left, there is a footpath sign. Turn right here and go along the left-hand side of the hedge all the way up to the trees where the path turns sharp left and goes up to a stile by a gate.

3. Cross the stile in front of you (ignore the turning on your right) and walk over the field towards the church tower. Go through the kissing gate at the other side and follow the paved path through the immaculate churchyard and past the right-hand side of St Mary's. This takes you onto the road which you continue along past the entrance to the Manor House on your right and up to the bridge over the stream. Turn right just before this bridge through a gate and then immediately turn right again through another gate. Go left and walk up the middle of the field between the stream on your left and a line of mixed trees on your right. These surround the Manor House and the old motte and bailey castle. At the end go through the kissing gate, turn right and follow the path over the stream and up to the road. Turn right and the Chequers is immediately on your left.

⑮ St Leonards
The White Lion

The Chilterns do not always mean hard hill walking. Here on the remarkably flat plateau only a few undulations break up what is otherwise a gentle stroll through pleasant fields and woods. Despite the isolation there are notable features to look out for like the startling white church at St Leonards and the replica drawbridge at Dundridge Manor.

Despite the close proximity of the ancient Icknield Way and Grim's Ditch there was probably no settlement here until after the Norman Conquest. Local legend has it that a hermit called Leonard of Blakemore rented an acre of grass and an acre of corn here and it was he who founded the church in the 12th century. What is known is that this strip at the top of the Chilterns was used as a source of wood and summer pasture for the villages in the vale below. Despite the ever encroaching suburbia, St Leonards is still remarkably remote with isolated groups of modest houses sprinkled around rolling fields and clumps of woodland.

This is very much the case with the White Lion which stands alone half a mile from the centre of the village. The long white building is 17th century in origin and the rustic tiled roof and little dormer windows complete its period look. Inside, this is maintained by the low-beamed ceiling and wood panelling. To your right is a large beam overhanging the recessed fireplace with illuminated nooks in the surrounding brickwork, while to the left the ceiling is raised to give an airy eating area. Blackboards adorn the walls, listing a good selection of meals like Yorkshire ham, battered cod, bangers and mash and vegetarian lasagne. Sandwiches and sweets are also on offer. Behind the bar are handpumps serving Marston's Pedigree and Benskins, along with wines, spirits, malts and cider. To the side of the pub is a secluded garden area which is completely surrounded by a hedge and offers a safe haven for children. This pretty and welcoming local also claims to be the highest pub in the Chilterns! The opening hours are 11 am to 2.30 pm and 6 pm to 11 pm (10.30 pm on Sunday); no meals on Sunday evening.

Telephone: 01494 758387.

- **HOW TO GET THERE:** From Aylesbury take the A41 towards Tring and after a few miles enter Aston Clinton. Just past the roundabout next to the Rising Sun turn right up the B489, over the canal bridge and up to the T junction. Turn right towards Wendover and then first left, signposted to St Leonards. Follow the road for about 3 miles, past the little white church, round a few bends and then you suddenly come across the White Lion on your left.
- **PARKING:** The only place to park safely is in the gravel car park to the side of the pub. There are a few spaces around Buckland Common if you are unable to park by the pub.
- **LENGTH OF THE WALK:** 2½ miles (3½ miles if you carry on up to the Ridgeway). Maps: OS Explorer 181 (formerly 2) Chiltern Hills North or Landranger 165 Aylesbury and Leighton Buzzard (GR 918069).

THE WALK

1. At the rear of the car park where it meets the hedge around the pub garden is a stile. Start the walk by crossing this and continue down the middle of the field to the gate at the bottom. Go over the stile next to it, then cross the one on the other side of the road and walk up the field to the stile and gate at the top. Over this, turn left up the road, past a white house and then as the road bends right go across the stile in front of you. Carry on in the same direction over the field to a gap in the hedge

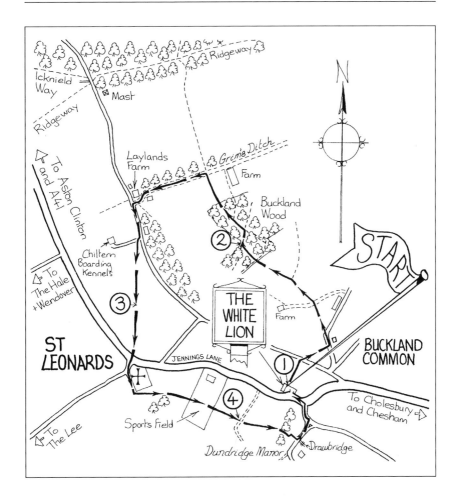

on the other side. Cross the track and stile on the other side and walk up the right-hand side of the next field to the top corner. Note the pits littered around these fields which were probably dug to extract clay for local brickworks. There are a number of local cottages with 'Kiln' in their name and there is still a working brickworks near Cholesbury.

Go over the stile in the corner and cross the middle of the next field (towards the second from the left pole in the further of the two electricity lines) where as you pass you will find a stile on the edge of the wood. Over this you carry on in the same direction through the trees until you shortly reach the other side and a T junction with another path.

73

St Leonards Church

2. Turn right down along the edge of the wood and then back into the trees where you come to a post and crossroads of paths. Take the left-hand one which leads you up the middle of the wood, past another post (keep to the left-hand path) and up to the top where you go over the stile. Walk along the right-hand side of the short field on the other side up to the track. This track runs along the remains of the ancient Grim's Ditch which is believed to date back more than 2,000 years and was probably used to mark a boundary. (To extend the walk, you could go straight on here up to the Ridgeway, turn left along it and then return along the road to Laylands Farm.)

For the main walk, go left and follow the track to Laylands Farm where you turn left along the road. You quickly come across a pretty semi-detached house set in the wood on your left, while on the other side is a drive leading down to Chiltern Boarding Kennels. Go over the stile on the left-hand side of the driveway entrance and diagonally down the field, cross the stile at the bottom and walk up the next field in the same direction.

3. Go through the hedge at the top and carry on over this field to a stile which puts you on the road by a T junction. Cross the road and start down the lane opposite and then first left down a drive by the right side of the picturesque white church. This leads between a garage and the churchyard, then turns left at the end of the latter and over a stile into the field. Cross this diagonally towards the left of the large oaks ahead and behind them you will find another stile. In the next field turn slightly right and go straight over to the stile in the hedge opposite. Now you carry on in the same direction across firstly a sports field, then another arable one which leads you up to a concrete drive.

4. Go over this and the stile opposite, then turn slightly to your left before crossing the next field to the trees on the other side. Over the next stile, turn slightly left and walk across to the gate in the hedge. Through this you find yourself on a drive with a drawbridge in front of you! This is only a replica but the moat it crosses is original and still surrounds Dundridge Manor.

Turn left and walk up the tree-lined drive, and then up the left-hand fork to the road. Turn left and walk along this side of the road round a sharp right bend and up to a T junction. Turn left and the White Lion is straight in front of you.

16 Little Hampden
The Rising Sun

This route passes through classic Chiltern woodland and well-grazed grass slopes. There are numerous views over unspoilt valleys, isolated hamlets and glimpses of the red-brick Chequers. More unusual is the mixed variety of flora in the landscape; it's not all beech trees, there is even some heathland more typical of Surrey.

There are few more secluded spots in the Chilterns than Little Hampden. Hidden at the end of a winding lane, this tiny enclave of cottages and a pub seems to have been cut out of the surrounding woodland. The opposite is more likely as a picture in the pub shows that seventy years ago this was open commonland and most of the encroaching trees have grown in recent times as grazing ceased. Although the village was part of the Hampden Estate the more notable local house is Chequers. This Elizabethan mansion was restored at the turn of the 20th century and given to the nation by Lord Lee as a country retreat for the Prime Minister. Each leader has maintained a tradition of planting a tree in the grounds; the avenue of beeches along the main drive was Winston Churchill's contribution.

The Rising Sun is comprised of two brick houses linked together at the far end of the village. Although both sides look of the same age the left-hand side is recent, but has been thoughtfully constructed in the same chequered brick pattern as its 200-year-old twin. Inside you are confronted by a central bar which seems caged in by old beams. The left-hand bar has a large fireplace with blackboards above listing the impressive and ever-changing menu. To the right are two more seating areas; the rear is especially snug with its low ceiling. Handpumps dispense Adnams, Brakspear and Pedigree, while there is also a good collection of wines, spirits and some cider. Food is the main attraction of the pub with beautifully prepared and presented meals including snacks and vegetarian choices. The picturesque setting along with the imaginative cuisine makes the Rising Sun well worth seeking out. The opening hours are 11.30 am to 3 pm and 6.30 pm to 10 pm on Monday to Saturday and 12 noon to 3 pm on Sunday (closed on Sunday evenings).

Telephone: 01494 488393/488360.

- **HOW TO GET THERE:** Leave the A413 Wendover to Amersham road at the roundabout halfway between the two and go down the road signposted to Great Missenden. At the mini roundabout at the end of the High Street turn right, go over a second mini roundabout and up to the top of the hill where you take the left fork for Princes Risborough. After a few miles out of the town the road takes a sharp left turn then goes right and passes through a tunnel of trees. At the end of this are two right-hand turns, the second of which is signposted to Little Hampden. Go up here and follow the winding narrow lane all the way up the hill, past the houses and at the very end the Rising Sun will appear on your left.
- **PARKING:** There are spaces next to and opposite the pub.
- **LENGTH OF THE WALK:** 3 miles (but feels more with the rolling countryside.) Maps: OS Explorer 181 (formerly 2) Chiltern Hills North or Landranger 165 Aylesbury and Leighton Buzzard (GR 857040).

THE WALK

1. With your back to the Rising Sun turn left and walk up the lane past the end of the pub (ignore the track to your right) and just past the last house is a path forking off to your left. Go up here for 100 yards or so and then follow the main bridleway as it turns sharp left, round a slight

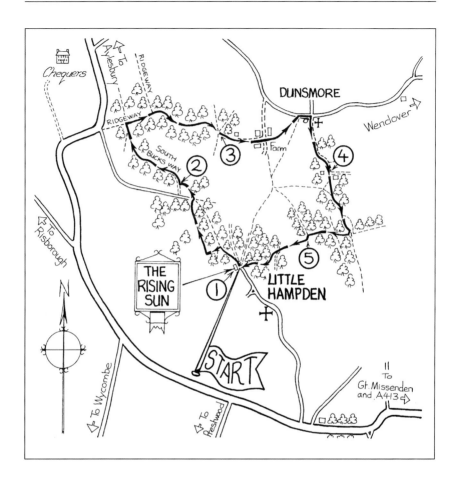

bend and out of the wood. Turn right at the top of this field and follow the edge of the wood (Icknield Way) until you reach the top corner of the next field. Through the gap in the trees is the top of a lane and crossroads of routes. Turn slightly to your left and take the path, South Bucks Way, which heads off through the trees from the right-hand side of the lane. Follow the blue arrows on the trees round a bend then turn right when it joins a wider path.

2. The path bends round to the left and back into woodland which you wander through; then as you enter some open scrub the path bends to the right and leads you slowly downhill. Near the bottom there is a crossroads of paths and you turn right up the Ridgeway to the top of the steep slope. Here the Ridgeway turns off to the left but you

other side past two trees on your left. This takes you up to a corner where you cross the stile and then, just before the gate which stands on a bend in a road, you turn right and head down the path between the trees. This takes you down, round a slight right bend and onto the tarmac drive. Turn left and walk down the drive until it takes a left turn and you fork off to the right by a footpath marker post.

4. This path takes you through a wood until a track joins from the left and you come out of the trees. Ignore the track, go slightly to your left past an arrow on a post and walk along the left-hand side of the hedge as it twists left and right down to the road at the bottom.

Turn right, go up the road a few yards and then turn left up the first lane where, after only a short distance, you turn right up a track lined with stones. The house you pass here on your right has Queen Anne-style rounded gables which are similar to the ones on the building to the left of the pub and another one you will see later along the main road in Penn, both dating back nearly 300 years. Go through the gap in the hedge and carry on up the track which runs along the bottom of the dry valley and past two round clumps of trees up on your left. These cover old pits which were possibly dug for chalk to marl the fields or for clay for making bricks or tiles.

5. At the top you reach a hedge where what is now but a path goes right up along the hedge but you carry straight on through it and along the hedge on your left up to the wood. Go along the bottom of this and then turn left up its other side (follow the horseshoe signs) and walk up this slope in a straight line until, passing through the gate at the top, you come onto the main road. Turn right and follow the pavement all the way back to the Rising Sun, passing on your way a beautiful old garage with MGs and other classic cars for sale, and a couple of quaint bookshops.

18 Frieth
The Yew Tree

The beautiful countryside proves incentive enough to do this walk. The view as you descend out of the woods to Fingest is picture postcard quality and the village itself never disappoints. The mix of woodland and pasture make this an inspiring circuit whatever the season.

This pretty hilltop village is made up of an attractive mix of brick, flint and timber cottages and a humble church standing in front of a trim green. It overlooks one of the most attractive parts of the Chilterns, the Hambledon Valley, and this walk also visits Fingest which stands at the head of it. The massive Norman church tower dominates this village and would have been familiar to Henry de Burghers, the Bishop of Lincoln who owned the manor in the 14th century. He enraged locals by fencing off part of the surrounding countryside which included their commonland but when he died his ghost was cursed with having to look after it for eternity. The new Bishop of Lincoln despatched one of his 'Ghost Busters' who had all the boundaries removed and hence released the old Bishop from his torture!

Back in Frieth the main way through the fence which surrounds the Yew Tree is under the very tree from which the pub is named! This leads you to a large and surprisingly secluded patio area with numerous tables surrounded by shrubs and flowers. The building looks suitably rusticated with a red-brick front and tiled roof. Inside, this antique aura is enhanced with warm terracotta-coloured walls, a low ceiling and many interesting features. Behind the bar you will find Brakspear and London Pride and a good range of wines and spirits. Although the pub is known for its restaurant it still offers a good selection of bar snacks, displayed on a blackboard above the fireplace. There can be few better feelings than sitting down in the garden here after a good walk and soaking up the peaceful surroundings and your favourite tipple! The opening hours are 10.30 am to 2.30 pm and 5.30 pm to 11 pm (10.30 pm on Sunday).

Telephone: 01494 882330.

- **HOW TO GET THERE:** From junction 4 on the M40 take the A4010 towards Aylesbury and after two roundabouts the road curves round to the right and you come to a third one by a garage and shops. Turn left here and follow the road for about a mile, over the motorway, past Booker Garden Centre and up to a T junction with the B482. Turn right and after a few dips the road enters Lane End. At the top of the hill just past the Clayton Arms turn left and keep to this road all the way to Frieth. As you enter the village you will find the Yew Tree on your right.

- **PARKING:** There is a large car park to the side of the pub or you can park along the roadside, the best place being further up the hill past the church.

- **LENGTH OF THE WALK:** $3^{1}/_{2}$ miles. Maps: OS Explorer 171 Chiltern Hills West (formerly 3 Chiltern Hills South) or Landranger 175 Reading and Windsor (GR797902).

THE WALK

1. With your back to the pub turn right and walk up the road past the church and turn right by the black timber building down Innings Road. Follow this past some houses on your left until the road makes a sharp right turn and you continue straight on down the track. This again turns right after a few hundred yards but you carry on down the tree-lined path in front of you. Keep to this path as it dips and then bends to the right (ignoring the left-hand turn) and brings you up to a stile.

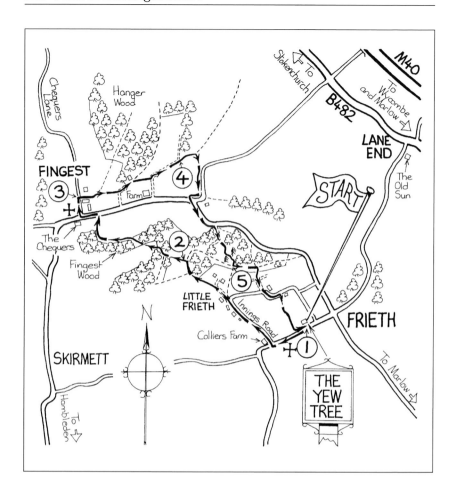

2. Turn left in front of this and walk along the track which follows the edge of the wood before entering it properly. The land to your right is more like scrub, probably due to storm damage over the past decades. The track bends right then left and brings you up to a gate. Go round this and turning 20 degrees right head across the field towards the wood on your right. Here you will find by a wooden sign a gap which you pass through and then, turning slightly left, go down the straight path to the gate at the other side of the wood. From this gate is one of the best views in the county!

Go over the stile next to the gate, walk past the seat and along the top of the field, going right as the wood turns downhill, and then over a

The view from Fingest Wood

stile by a gate before reaching the road at the bottom. Turn left along the road into Fingest. The massive church tower is nearly 900 years old and is so wide that it had to be covered by a twin roof. The Chequers pub opposite makes an excellent halfway house.

Take your first right up Chequers Lane, past the telephone box, and then just behind the timber and brick cottage at right angles to the road (Church Cottage) turn right down the footpath.

3. The footpath runs between a fence and brick wall and takes you up to the edge of a field. Take the right-hand path here (straight on in effect) along the fence and over the next stile. Continue along the fence in the field beyond up to and over the stile in the corner. Turn left up the track and as you climb the hill the trees close in and you come across a fork in the track (beside some storage sheds). Take the right-hand footpath which runs level along the edge of the wood and up to another track. Turn left and then follow it round a sharp right-hand bend and straight down through some sheep pens to the bottom right corner of the field.

4. Go over the stile in the corner and along the hedge on your right until after a few hundred yards it bends 90 degrees and you do the

87

same right turn up to and over the next stile. This leads you up to a bend on a road where you turn right and walk along the right-hand side past a seat (with another good view), round another right-hand bend and down to a T junction. Turn left up the road signposted Frieth and Marlow, keeping to the path on the right-hand side, until you reach the wood. Turn right through the gate by the footpath sign in the bottom corner of this wood and walk up the track between the trees. This shortly turns right (and was taped off when I walked here) so you carry straight on up the path which is well marked by painted white arrows on the trees. Look out for these arrows as this is still a working wood and felling may make the path obscure at times. This same felling and storm damage has allowed some flowers and grasses to become established in the clearings, making a change from the usually bare beechwoods.

The path twists and turns through the wood and then some conifers before turning sharp right and coming up to a crossroads of paths by a post.

5. Turn left and follow this wider track as it drops slightly over the next few hundred yards until you come to another post and crossroads by a recently felled area. Turn right up to a wire fence, then turning to your right walk along its edge up to the end of an unmade road. Go up this road (ignoring the driveways to your left and right) and you come to the corner of a tarmac road. Turn left in front of some pretty cottages and follow the road as it turns left down a narrow steep hill. Halfway down on the right is a footpath sign and a stile which you cross; walk between the hedge and fence up to the corner of this first field. Follow the path as it turns round to the left and leads you up to and over another stile. Now continue up the right-hand side of the long narrow field beyond and over the stile in its top corner. This takes you between the houses and back to the road. Turn left and you will shortly be back outside the Yew Tree.

19 **Bourne End**
The Garibaldi

*This walk offers a mix of the differing landscapes that connect the
older parts of the Wooburn parish. You start in parkland dominated by
a folly and a church, climb up through woodland of oak and ash, then
return through the pretty houses of Wooburn and back along the disused
railway. There are fine views and two good pubs en route should you
need a refresher!*

In the early 19th century this southern part of the parish of Wooburn
was made up of the hamlets of Bone End, Cores End and Bourne End,
with a string of paper mills along the River Wye being the focus of
employment. Of greater importance then was Hedsor Wharf on the
River Thames which had, for centuries, been the main loading point for
goods from Wycombe bound for London. In 1830 a new lock was built
at Cookham, bypassing the wharf and this dangerous stretch of the
river. Lord Boston who owned the wharf and the towing rights claimed
compensation for loss of business but it was not until 1894 that it was
finally settled and he had ownership of this section of the river

confirmed. This made it the only part of the main river in private hands. The wharf had previously closed and was eventually made into one large residence in 1971 for Tiny Rowland.

Across the fields and trapped between rows of Victorian cottages stands the Garibaldi. The whitewashed exterior covers the rich, red brickwork which is still exposed at the rear. Inside, the tidy interior is well decorated with fake but atmospheric beams, plush carpet and an ample sprinkling of cushions. There is a small glass-roofed eating area at the back and some table and chairs on the patios at the front and rear. Inside is served Speckled Hen, Draught Bass and a regular guest beer, alongside cider, wines, spirits and a few malts. This is a welcomingly peaceful and unpretentious pub blessed with long opening hours and a good, varied menu. It is open from 11.30 am to 3 pm and 5.30 pm to 11 pm on Monday to Thursday, 11.30 am to 11 pm on Friday and Saturday and 12 noon to 10.30 pm on Sunday. Telephone: 01628 522092.

- **HOW TO GET THERE:** From junction 4 on the M40 take the A404 towards Maidenhead and then just before the bottom of the hill take the first turning off and go left down the A4155 for Bourne End. At the roundabout at the end of the parade of shops take the right-hand fork which is the A4094 to Cookham. Go past the Walnut Tree pub, round a sharp left bend and turn immediately left along the road signposted to Hedsor. The Garibaldi is about 1/4 mile down on the left.

- **PARKING:** There is a small car park to the rear of the pub, accessed through the archway. If you prefer to park on the road then the best place will be opposite the garden centre before the pub, as spaces are limited around the Garibaldi.

- **LENGTH OF THE WALK:** 4 miles (including an optional walk up to St Nicholas's church). Maps: OS Explorer 172 Chiltern Hills East (formerly 3 Chiltern Hills South) or Landranger 175 Reading and Windsor (GR 900866).

THE WALK

1. With your back to the pub turn left and head up the slightly rising road until the last house on the right where there is a footpath sign by a track. Go across the field in the direction of the sign, up to the road. Turn right and walk along the right-hand verge until the road starts to dip and you cross and use the left-hand side down to the bottom of the dip. Here you turn left up the private drive signposted to Priory

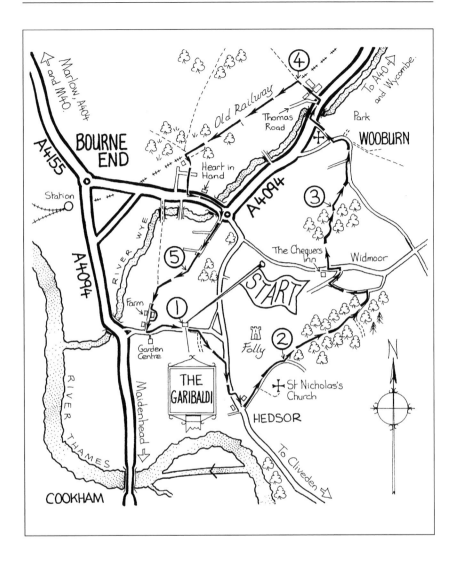

Nurseries. Halfway up on your right is a steep path up to St Nicholas's, a pretty church blessed with fine views. On the opposite side on top of the hill is Lord Boston's Folly. It was built in the 18th century to be an eyecatching feature from his house beyond the church. It was cleverly converted into a house with a low level round base in 1992.

Carrying on up the drive takes you round a right bend and up to a white gate.

91

2. Here you fork left and follow the footpath marked 'Beeches Way' which takes you up the hill between the fences lined with horse chestnut, oak, ash and yews! At the top of the hill it emerges on a track where you turn left (virtually straight ahead) and continue up to a very minor road. Turn left and at the next T junction turn right past the houses of Harvest Hill to another junction. Go left and just before the Chequers Inn (an excellent halfway house) there is a stile on the right-hand side of the road. Go over this and cross straight over the field and into the wood by the stile. The path meanders down through the wood of oak, ash and beech until you emerge above Wooburn with excellent views up and down the Wye Valley.

3. Cross the field ahead by turning 30 degrees right and going towards the last red-brick house to the right of the church where you will find a stile. Go over it and turn left along the fence then drop down onto the road and continue down into the village. You shortly go round a sharp left bend and then just before the church turn right and go up to the main road. Just past the church on the main road is the site of an old hotel, now a housing estate, which was used for all the external shots in *Fawlty Towers!* Cross over and turn right along the River Wye and then just past the entrance to Thomas Road turn left up a footpath which goes up the right-hand side of the row of cottages.

4. The path ends at some gates across the old railway and you turn left and follow the old track along the rear of the industrial and housing estates and then through more pleasant pastures. As the trees close in and just before the first house on your left there is a crossroads of paths. Turn left past the 'Nature Walk' sign and along the back of the houses, over the end of a close and down to the main road. Turn left and follow the A4094 past the Heart in Hand pub, over the River Wye and then cross over just before the roundabout and go right, down Princes Road. Carry straight on, ignoring the two right-hand turns, and just after the last you emerge onto a field. Go along the right-hand side and up to a kissing gate.

5. Turn slightly to your right and carry on over the next field towards the corner at the left-hand end of the industrial buildings. Go through the kissing gate (ignoring the gap and gate on your right) and walk along the right-hand side of the next field. Beyond the next gate is a concrete road through the field. The path goes through a gate on your left, curves around the back of the cowshed and rejoins the concrete road on the other side. Carry on along this up to the road, where you turn left to return to the Garibaldi.

20 Taplow
The Oak and Saw

This area must have been witness to many historic figures and events. There is the burial mound of a Saxon prince, just below which is Maidenhead Bridge, a crossing place for many a king or queen, and beside it Brunel's Bridge which carries one of the first great main line railways. Linking all of these is the River Thames which has been a thoroughfare itself since Neolithic times.

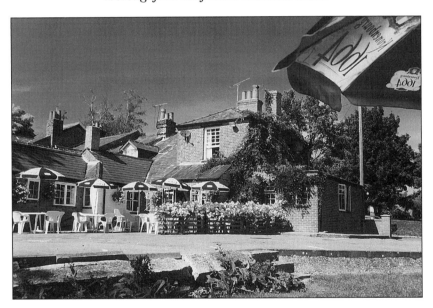

In 1883 the mysterious mound which stood in the grounds of Taplow Court was opened. As the excavators dug lower they came across a timber-lined area within which were the remains of a man clothed in a gold embroidered garment. Around him were weapons, shields, a harp, drinking horns with bronze and silver mounts, glass beakers, a great gold buckle and thirty gaming counters in case he became bored on his journey to the Next World. The man is believed to be the Saxon Prince Taeppa who gives the village its name (the 'low' part means mound or promontory). This was, until the discovery of the Sutton Hoo ship burial in Suffolk, the richest Saxon find in the country and it still warrants a separate display area in the British Museum. Until 1828 the mound had stood within the grounds of the medieval church. The present church, resited when Taplow Court was extended, mainly dates from 1911, making it much younger than the early 19th century Oak and Saw which stands opposite.

The attractive chequered brick exterior of the pub, clad on one side by climbers, is made all the more picturesque by the setting among period houses, the church and green. The interior is one simple bar area with an eating section to the right and the entrance to the garden and patio straight ahead. Three handpumps dispense 6X, Rebellion IPA and Pedigree and the food on offer is refreshingly down to earth, for example the 'Oak and Saw Burger', vegetarian cannelloni and fish steaks. At the rear there is a hard patio area while on the other side of the car park is a small grass triangle which commands views down the gently sloping fields to the Thames. The opening hours are 12 noon to 3 pm and 5.30 pm to 11 pm from Monday to Wednesday and 12 noon to 11 pm on Thursday to Saturday. Sunday hours are 12 noon to 3.30 pm and 5.30 pm to 10.30 pm.

Telephone: 01628 604074.

- **HOW TO GET THERE:** From junction 2 on the M40 take the A355 towards Slough but after a few hundred yards take the first right, signposted to Burnham. Follow this road for a few winding miles until just past the Jolly Woodsman pub and the little church you turn right up Wooburn Common Road. After $1/4$ mile turn left down Heathfield Road and continue for just over 2 miles past Cliveden until, passing along a length of the road lined with tall trees, there is Hill Farm Road forking off to the left. Go down here, into the village, and then turn right along either High Street or Rectory Road, both of which lead to the Oak and Saw.
- **PARKING:** There is a large car park to the rear but also ample space along the roads in front.
- **LENGTH OF THE WALK:** $3^1/2$ miles ($4^1/2$ miles if you carry on along the Thames to Bray Lock). Maps: OS Explorer 172 Chiltern Hills East (formerly 3 Chiltern Hills South) or Landranger 175 Reading and Windsor (GR 911821).

THE WALK

1. With your back to the pub turn left and walk up Rectory Road past the Old Rectory with its collection of painted wheel covers, and on up

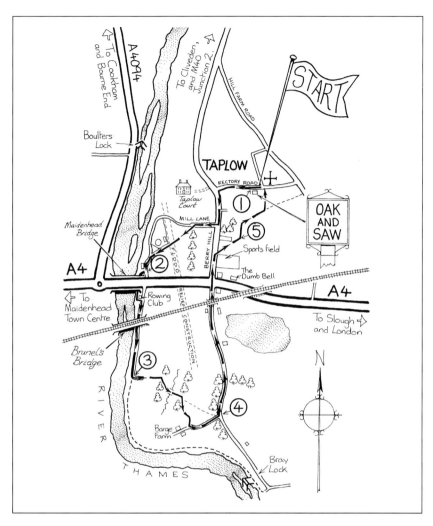

to Berry Hill. Turn left down the road, past Saxon Gardens, and then turn right up Mill Lane. Just past the last house on the right the road narrows and there is a footpath forking off to the left. Go down here, heading towards the left-hand side of the gasometer. At the time of writing a new flood relief channel was being dug across this point. There will be a bridge crossing here but there may be some disruption further along the walk in the coming year or so.) The tarmac path goes past the gasometer and ends at the bend in a road. Turn left and go round the bend and up towards the A4.

2. Just before you reach the A4 there is a Thames Path sign which leads you right through a small boatyard and under the first arch of Maidenhead Bridge. There has been a bridge across the Thames here since the 12th century but the present magnificent Georgian crossing was completed in 1777. On the other side the path passes in front of a rowing club then immediately after the building you turn left and walk through the car park and onto the road.

Turn right and continue under Brunel's Bridge. The main span is the widest and flattest brick arch of its date in the world at 128 ft in length. It was built in 1838 to carry Brunel's new broad gauge Great Western Railway and the bridge features in Turner's painting *Rain, Steam and Speed.*

After this bridge the road passes some grand, mainly 20th-century houses until, just after a gate, the now gravel drive turns sharp left and goes between the last two houses. (If you wish to lengthen the walk, then you can continue along the path through the trees ahead and follow the river all the way to Bray Lock, just past which you can pick up the track which leads back to point 4.)

3. Go left up between the houses and past the garage and stables on your right. Continue along the fence between the fields up to the trees where the path becomes a track. Follow this for the next $1/2$ mile as it bends first right then left, through hedgerows and eventually past a house and disused farm buildings until it meets a gravel track. (The actual footpath is meant to cross the field here as marked on the map but was virtually invisible when I walked it so I kept to the tracks.) Turn left away from the farm, around a couple of bends and up to another T junction of tracks.

4. Turn left and follow this track through the fields, past the boating lake, under the railway bridge and up to the crossroads by the garage. Cross over the A4 and go straight up Berry Hill opposite, along the pavement on the right-hand side. Just past the end of the sports field is a kissing gate on your right which you pass through and then head up between the two clumps of trees and on in the same direction to the top corner of the field.

5. Go through the kissing gate and up the path between the fence on your left and the hedge on your right. At the end you pass through another gate, then turn 45 degrees right and cross the field to the hedge on the other side where you find another kissing gate. Go through this and up the tree-lined path which puts you back on Rectory Road beside the church and pub.